D0395107

SEARCHING FOR
Anne Frank

Designer: Allison Henry

Library of Congress Cataloging-in-Publication Data

Rubin, Susan Goldman.
Searching for Anne Frank : letters from Amsterdam to Iowa / by Susan
Goldman Rubin in collaboration with the Simon Wiesenthal Center Museum
of Tolerance Library and Archives.
p. cm.
Summary: Provides a glimpse of life during World War II in both the
Netherlands and the United States through the correspondence of Anne
Frank and her Iowa pen pals.
ISBN 0-8109-4514-2
1. Frank, Anne, 1929-1945. 2. Frank, Anne, 1929–1945—Correspondence—Juvenile literature.
3. Jews—Netherlands—Amsterdam—Biography—Juvenile literature. 4. Jewish
children in the Holocaust—Netherlands—Amsterdam—Biography—Juvenile
literature. 5. Holocaust, Jewish (1939–1945)—Netherlands—Amsterdam—Juvenile literature.
6. Wagner, Juanita. 7. Heibner, Betty. 8. School children—Iowa—Biography—Juvenile literature.
9. School children—Iowa—Correspondence—Juvenile literature. [1. Frank, Anne,
1929–1945. 2. Jews—Netherlands. 3. Holocaust, Jewish
(1939–1945)—Netherlands—Amsterdam. 4. Wagner, Juanita. 5. Heibner,
Betty. 6. Women—Biography. 7. Netherlands—History—German occupation,
1940–1945. 8. World War, 1939–1945—United States.] I. Museum of
Tolerance (Simon Wiesenthal Center) II. Title.
DS135.N6.F73556 2003
940.53'18'092—dc21

Harry N. Abrams, Inc.
100 Fifth Avenue
New York, N.Y. 10011
www.abramsbooks.com

Abrams is a subsidiary of

LA MARTINIÈRE
G R O U P E

SEARCHING FOR
Anne Frank

LETTERS *from* AMSTERDAM *to* IOWA

by SUSAN GOLDMAN RUBIN

IN ASSOCIATION WITH THE SIMON WIESENTHAL CENTER—
MUSEUM OF TOLERANCE LIBRARY AND ARCHIVES

HARRY N. ABRAMS, INC., PUBLISHERS

contents

ONE

Iowa, 1939–1940

In the fall of 1939, Juanita Jane Wagner picked a name from a list of pen pals. Juanita, a ten-year-old student in Danville, Iowa, wanted to write to a girl her age who lived in Europe. Her teacher, Miss Birdie Mathews, loved to travel and had visited Holland (the Netherlands), Germany, Switzerland, and Italy in 1914, and had probably made the journey again during the summer of 1939. (Family memories differ.)

In those days most Americans did not travel abroad. They stayed where they had grown up. So when Miss Birdie took an "extended trip" to England and Scotland with a tour group during the summer of 1914, she made front-page news in the *Henry County Times*. The local paper, whose motto was "New London and Henry County First—the World Afterward," reprinted her letters home to her mother. Miss Birdie, as she was called at school, hoped to excite her students' curiosity in the world beyond their little American town by a pen-pal program.

At the end of her trip in 1939, Miss Birdie was stranded in Naples, Italy. Her steamer could not sail on schedule because a war was brewing. "The war cloud spreads and darkens all our days," wrote Miss

Juanita Jane Wagner, age eleven

Birdie in a poem as she waited to leave. "We rush about like badly frightened geese!" When her steamer finally set sail, she and other passengers were horrified to see a ship that suddenly disappeared from view. They wondered if it had been torpedoed by the Germans. If so, would they be hit next?

But Miss Birdie arrived home safely. During her travels, or perhaps at Columbia University in New York City where she sometimes took courses, she had met teachers from a Montessori school in Amsterdam. They gave Miss Birdie names and addresses of their students for a pen-pal project. Miss Birdie called it "my program of international correspondence" and looked forward to launching it with her sixth-, seventh-, and eighth-grade students.

When school opened in September 1939, World War II had begun in Europe. Six years previously Adolf Hitler, head of the National Socialist Party (Nazi, for short), had taken power in Germany and had established a dictatorship. He outlawed any political groups except his own and planned to get rid of people who opposed him or whom he did not like, especially Jews. He began a program of creating a master race, murdering German adults and children who were mentally and physically disabled. Hitler intended to conquer all of Europe and create a huge German empire. On September 1, 1939, he invaded Poland, and two days later Great Britain and France declared war on Germany.

Miss Birdie Mathews, around 1940

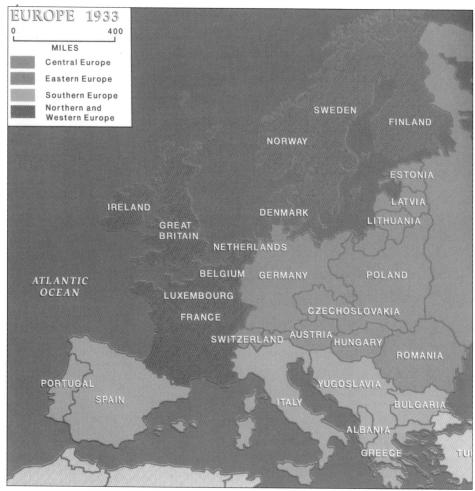

Map of Europe in 1933

Although Americans felt sympathetic toward European countries, they did not want to get involved. A committee called America First was formed to keep the United States out of the war. Some of its members were antisemitic (prejudiced against Jews) and unjustly blamed the Jews for all America's misfortunes. The committee gathered much support in the Midwest, where many Iowans considered themselves "isolationists." They figured they had enough trouble fighting nature: "drought, frost, wind, hail, green-fly . . . Why should men take on their own kind as well?" they said.

Despite the trouble in Europe and the debate over what, if any-

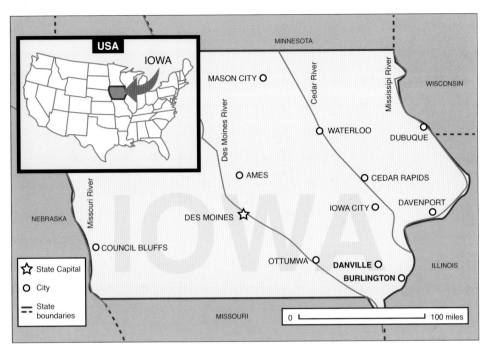

Map of Iowa showing Danville and Burlington

thing, to do about it, Miss Birdie gave her students the names and addresses of children to whom they could write. Juanita and her class-mates Kathleen and Betty Heibner selected girls who lived in Holland. Kathleen sent a gift hankie with her letter to Bea Popping in Amsterdam. Juanita also chose a pen pal who lived in Amsterdam. Her name was Anne Frank.

Juanita had no idea that Anne was Jewish. There were no Jews in Danville, but religious differences did not matter to Juanita and her family. Their small community of 309 people attended five different churches. The Wagners belonged to the Methodist Church.

In her letter to Anne, Juanita told her about Danville. She asked Anne to try to find it on a map of the United States. "It's near Burlington," she explained, "a bigger city located on the Mississippi River."

Juanita also wrote about her family and life on the farm. Her name, unusual for an Iowa girl, had come from the title of an old song that was one of her mother's favorites. Her mother even called her "Nita," for short, just like the words of the refrain:

9

Nita! Juanita!

Let me linger by thy side!

Juanita's father had died when Juanita was only four years old and now she, her fourteen-year-old sister, Betty, and their mother raised crops of corn, oats, and soybeans with the assistance of "renters." The girls helped with farm chores and took care of the chickens. Barefoot and bareback, they rode their horse, Prince, as he pulled the hay wagon. Sometimes they rode Prince to school, three miles away. To make ends meet, their mother taught at Possum Hollow, a one-room country school.

Juanita waited eagerly for a reply. She received her first of two letters from Anne in February or early March. On March 5, 1940, the school newspaper, *The Danvillian*, reported this item in "Grade News" about Fifth and Sixth: "Juanita Wagner and Betty Heibner have received answers to their letters sent to Holland. One girl wrote that she had had only three months of English, and a very amusing expression that she used was, 'The tears walked down our cheeks.'"

And news for Seventh and Eighth opened: "Several of us have received answers to our letters which we sent to Holland. . . . We painted pictures of windmills and Dutch boys Friday."

But Kathleen's pen pal, Bea, corrected a false impression of how Dutch boys and girls dressed. "We don't walk on wooden shoes," she wrote, "and we don't wear old fashioned costumes, only in some parts of the country."

Miss Birdie's souvenir flyer from her trip on the
Steamboat Antoinette from Amsterdam to Edam

Juanita's only letter from Anne that exists was dated April 29, 1940. Like Bea, she wrote in English. It is believed that Anne's first draft was in Dutch, and then her father, Otto Frank, translated the words and had her redo the letter in English. Anne also enclosed a letter from her four-teen-year-old sister, Margot, addressed to Juanita's sister, Betty; photographs of themselves; and a picture postcard. Anne wrote:

Photograph of Anne, almost ten, May 1939, sent to Juanita

Dear Juanita,

I did receive your letter and want to answer you as quick as possible. Margot and myself are the only children in our house. Our grandma is living with us. My father has an office and mother is busy at home. I have [sic]* not far from school and I am sitting in the fifth class. We have no hour-classes we may do what we prefer, of course we must get to a certain goal. Your mother will certainly know this system, it is called Montessori. We have little work at home.

On the map I looked again and found the name Burlington. I did ask a girl friend of mine if she would like to communicate with one of your friends. She wants to do it with a girl about my age not with a boy.

I shall write her address underneath. Did you yourself write the letter I received from you, or did your mother do it? I include a post-card from Amsterdam and shall continue to do that collecting picture-cards I have already about 800. A child I used to be at school with went to New-York and she did write a letter to our class some time ago. In case you and Betty get a photo do send a copy as I am curious to know how you look. My birthday is the 12th of June. Kindly let me know yours. Perhaps one of your friends wil [sic] write first to my girl friend, for she also cannot write English but her father or mother will translate the letter.

Hoping to hear from you I remain
your Dutch friend
Annelies Marie Frank

*sic *indicates text is reproduced as it originally appeared, often acknowledging an error*

Dear Juanita, I Amsterdam 29 april Monday.

I did receive your letter and want to answer you as quick as possible. Margot and myself are the only children in our house. Our grandma is living with us. My father has an office and mother is busy at home. I have not far from school and I am sitting in the fifth class. We have no hour-classes we may do what we prefer, of course we must get to a certain goal. Your mother will certainly know this system, it is called Montessori. We have little work at home.

On the map I looked again and found the name Burlington. I did ask a girl friend of mine if she would like to communicate with one of your friends. She wants to do it with a girl about my age not with a boy.

I shall write her address underneath. Did you yourself write the letter I received from you, or did your mother do it? I include a post-card from Amsterdam and shall continue to do that collecting picture-cards I have already about 800. A child I used to be at school with went to New-York and she did with a letter to our class some time ago. In case you and Betty get a photo do send a copy as. I am curious to know how you look My birthday is the 12th of June. Kindly let me know yours. Perhaps one of your friends will write first to my girl friend, for she also cannot write English but her father or mother will translate the letter.

Hoping to hear from you I remain

your Dutch friend
Annelies Marie Frank.

P.S. Please write me the address, of a girl.
The address of my friend is

Mej. Susanne Ledermann.
Noorder Amstellaan 37
Amsterdam (Zuid)
Nederland

Anne's letter to Juanita

In a postscript Anne wrote the name of her friend, Susanne Ledermann, and gave her address. And on the side of the letter she added Susanne's age: "old 11 years."

Anne's postcard showed a picture of a typical canal (*grachten* in Dutch), bordered by leafy trees. Her message read:

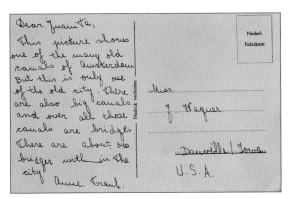

Back and front of Anne's picture postcard sent to Juanita

Dear Juanita,
    This picture shows one of the many old canals of Amsterdam. But this is only one of the old city. There are also big canals and over all those canals are bridges. There are about 340 bridges with in the city.
    Anne Frank

Margot's letter came in the same envelope marked "Miss J and B Wagner" and was dated 27 April 1940. She wrote:

Dear Betty Ann,

I have only received your letter about a week ago and had no time to answer right away. It is Sunday today, so I can take the time to write. During the week I am very busy as I have to work for school at home every day.

Our school begins at 9 a.m. till noon then I go home by my bicycle (if the weather is bad I go by bus and stay at school) and return for the class beginning at half past one; we then have clas [sic] until three o'clock. Wednesday and Saturday afternoon we are free and use our time to play tennis and to row. In the winter we play hockey or go skating if it is could [sic] enough. This year it was unusually cold and all the canals were frozen; today is the first really spring day, the sun shining bright and warm. Generally we have lot of rain.

In summer we have a two months holiday, then a fortnight at Christmas and so on Easter; Whitsuntide only four days.

Unlike Anne, Margot referred to the threatening situation in Europe. Just a couple of weeks earlier, on April 9, 1940, the Nazis had invaded Denmark and Norway.

We often listen to the radio, as times are very exciting, having a frontier with Germany and being a small country we never feel safe. In our class most of the

children communicate with one or the other so I do not know children who would want to take up correspon-dence. I only have two cousins, boy living at Basel, Switserland [sic]. For American ideas this is not far but for us it is. We have to travel through Germany which we cannot do or through Belgium and France and in that we cannot either. It is war and no visas are given.

We live in a five room flat attached to the only skyscraper of the city being twelve storey high! Amsterdam has about 800,000 inhabitants. We are near the sea shore but we miss hills and woods. Everything being flat and a great part of the country

Photograph of Margot, age thirteen, sent to Betty

Margot's letter to Betty

lying below sea level, therefore the name Netherland.

> *Father is going to business in the morning and returns about 6 p.m.; Mother is busy at home. My grand-mother is living with us and we rented one room to a lady.*
>
> *Now I think I have told you quite a lot and am expecting your answer.*
>
> *With kindest regards*
>
> *your friend*
>
> *Margot Betti Frank*
>
> *P.S. Many thanks for Juanita's letter as Anne is writing to her I need not write myself*
>
> *Margot*

Juanita and Betty were thrilled to hear from their Dutch pen pals. They wrote back immediately and sent snapshots of themselves. In eager anticipation they watched for their next letters from Anne and Margot.

TWO

amsterdam, 1940

While Betty and Juanita waited to hear from their pen pals, Anne and Margot Frank enjoyed life in Amsterdam despite the war that was going on in other parts of Europe. The Frank sisters lived at 37 Merwedeplein, a yellow brick building in the southern part of the city. Their spacious apartment on the third floor had central heating, a luxury in those days. As Margot wrote to Betty Ann, the row of buildings was attached to a "skyscraper," the first in Amsterdam.

Anne's best friends, Susanne (Sanne) Ledermann and Hannah (Hanneli) Elisabeth Goslar, lived in the same neighborhood. Hanneli's apartment building faced Anne's on the other side of a little park. And Sanne's apartment was around the corner on a main street leading into town. Anne and Hanneli attended the Montessori school a few blocks away. Sanne went to public school with her older sister, Barbara, and Anne's sister, Margot. Sanne wanted an American pen pal, too, and had asked Anne to give her name and address to Juanita.

Anne at the Montessori school, 1941

After school Anne, Sanne, and Hanneli played together every day. In her diary Anne wrote, "people who saw us together always said there they go Anne, Hanne and Sanne." They drew chalk lines on the sidewalk for a game of hopscotch, or played hide-and-seek, or turned cartwheels in the grassy park. Crossing the street was safe since there were few motorcars. Most people rode bikes. The flower seller came once a week in a cart pulled by a big dog, and the milkman made his deliveries in a horse-drawn wagon.

Sometimes the three friends just had fun giggling and telling secrets. "Anne was a girl like other girls her age," remembered Hanneli.

Anne, Sanne, and Hanneli had been friends for years. They were all Jewish refugees from Germany. Their families had emigrated to Holland in 1933 when Hitler and the Nazi Party seized power. Barbara and Sanne came from Berlin. Their father was

The Merwedeplein, Amsterdam. Franks' apartment: third floor, far right

a lawyer and their mother was a pianist. Through the children the parents met and became friends. On Sundays the Ledermanns gave chamber music recitals in their apartment, followed by refreshments, and all four of the Franks attended.

Anne and Margot had been born in Frankfurt. Their parents, Otto and Edith, belonged to rich, cultured families and considered themselves more German than Jewish. Otto rarely attended services at synagogue. Edith, however, was religious. Although they observed the holidays of *Yom Kippur* and *Pesach* (Passover), and celebrated *Hanukkah*, they also exchanged gifts at Christmas. But with the rise of antisemitism in Germany, the Franks knew they had to leave. Especially when their seven-year-old daughter Margot was not allowed to sit with non-Jewish children in school.

Otto's older brother, Robert, and his wife went to England. His

Anne's tenth birthday party, June 12, 1939. From left to right: Lucie van Dijk, Anne, Susanne (Sanne) Ledermann, Hannah (Hanneli) Goslar, Juultje Ketellapper, Kitty Egyedi, Mary Bos, Rie (Ietje) Swillens, and Martha van den Berg. Otto Frank took the picture on the sidewalk in front of the Franks' apartment building.

younger brother moved to France, and his mother, sister, and brother-in-law settled in Switzerland. Otto decided to take his wife and daughters to Holland, where he believed they would be safe. "In the Netherlands, after those experiences in Germany," he wrote, "it was as

Anne, age eight, plays in a neighbor's sandbox. From left to right: Hanneli, Anne, Dolly Citroen, Hannah Toby, Barbara Ledermann, and her sister, Sanne, 1937.

if our life was restored to us. Our children went to school and at least in the beginning our lives proceeded normally. In those days it was possible for us to start over and feel free."

Edith's family stayed in Germany until things grew worse. On November 9, 1938, the Nazis went on a rampage, burning synagogues and smashing Jewish-owned stores and houses. The riot was known as *Kristallnacht*, the night of broken glass. Soon afterward Edith's brothers, Walter and Julius Holländer, emigrated to America. And in 1939 their mother, Rosa, moved to Amsterdam to stay with the Franks. As Anne wrote to Juanita, "Our grandma is living with us."

In Amsterdam Otto established a branch of his family's business called Opekta. The company sold pectin, a substance used for making jam, and it also sold various seasonings and spices. At first the Opekta offices were located in a modern building near the center of the city. Then in December 1940 Otto transferred the business to number 263 on the Prinsengracht Canal. A young non-Jewish woman came to work for him. Her name was Miep Santrouschitz. Miep had been born in Vienna, Austria, but had grown up in Holland with a foster family and thought of herself as "a Dutch girl through and through."

From left: Barbara, Susanne (Sanne), and their parents, Franz and Ilse Ledermann.

Miep quickly developed a friendship with the Franks and often had dinner at their apartment. When she became engaged to Jan Gies, she introduced him to the Franks and he visited, too. They often discussed politics when the children were out of the room and shared a mutual hatred of the Nazi Party.

In the spring of 1940 Miep wrote, "Margot Frank turned fourteen . . . . We realized we were seeing a young lady rather than a girl. Anne clearly looked up to her older sister. Anything Margot did or said was sponged up by Anne's darting eyes and quick mind. In fact, Anne had developed the skill of mimicry. She would mimic anyone and anything, and very well at that; the cat's meow, her friend's voice, her teacher's authoritative tone."

Anne's parents purposely sent her to the Montessori school because they knew she needed a freer atmosphere than in an ordinary public school. "Anne was difficult," remembered Barbara Ledermann. "She couldn't sit still and loved to talk."

"It was good for Anne to go to a Montessori school," said Otto, "as every child was treated individually. . . . Anne was never a very good schoolgirl. She hated maths. I practised her times tables with her countless times. She only excelled in those subjects that interested her, particularly history."

Margot, on the other hand, was an excellent student. "Margot was the bright one," Otto recalled. "Everybody admired her. She got along with everybody."

Otto understood the differences between his daughters. "Anne was a normal, lively child who needed much tenderness and attention," he said, "and who delighted us and frequently upset us. When she entered a room, there was always a fuss. Anne never stopped asking questions. When we had visitors, she was so interested in them that it was hard to get rid of her."

Edith agreed. In a letter to a friend back in Germany, she wrote, "Anne is not so well behaved as Margot and does not like to buckle down to things. . . . Anne is struggling with her reading lessons."

Anne liked to have fun. She and Hanneli collected picture postcards, as she had told Juanita. They traded cards of the children in the Dutch and British royal families. Anne was also crazy about movies, especially American film stars. Her favorite cards featured pictures of Sonja Henie, the famous ice

Anne stands behind her teacher, Miss Gadron, in her Montessori classroom, 1940.

skater who had become an actress; Deanna Durbin; and Ray Milland. Anne dreamed of someday going to Hollywood.

Her interest in America may have been sparked by her father's experiences. Otto had lived in the United States for a short while before he was married. As a young man at Heidelberg University in Germany, he had become friends with an American student, Nathan Straus, Jr. Nathan's father owned Macy's department store in New York City. When Nathan's father offered Otto a job at the store, he accepted. Otto loved New York and learned much about business there; but when his own father died in 1909, he sailed home to Germany. Soon he returned to New York, however, and continued working at Macy's. With the outbreak of World War I, Otto went home again and enlisted in the army, but he and Nathan remained lifelong friends.

Edith Frank with Anne on the left and Margot on the right, Frankfurt, Germany, 1933. Photo taken by Otto Frank.

Anne was closer to her father than to her mother. She and Margot affectionately called him Pim. On Sundays Anne went to his office with her friend Hanneli and they played "secretaries," pretending to call each other on the office telephones.

Sometimes Edith took Anne and Margot to visit the many art museums in Amsterdam. They rode the trolley car into the center of the city and shopped for clothes at fashionable stores. But their normal life threatened to come to an end.

By spring 1940 Otto feared that Germany would attack neutral Holland. He wrote to his cousin Milly in England and said, "I don't know what to do about the children. I can't talk to Edith about it. There's no use worrying her before she has to be worried." Milly wrote back, "I know it sounds crazy, because we're at war and you're not. But if you think it's the least bit safe, please send the children here."

Otto answered, "Edith and I discussed your letter. We both feel we simply can't do it. We couldn't bear to part with the girls. They mean too much to us. But if it's any comfort to you, you are the people we would have trusted."

On May 10, 1940, just a couple of weeks after Anne and Margot had written to Juanita and Betty, the Nazis invaded the Netherlands, Belgium, Luxembourg, and France. The Dutch fought back, but four days later the

Members of Queen Wilhelmina's family: Crown Princess Juliana and Prince Bernhard with daughters Beatrix and Irene, late 1939

Netherlands surrendered to Germany. To avoid capture, Queen Wilhelmina and the royal family fled to England and there set up a Dutch government-in-exile. But the Franks and their friends remained in Amsterdam.

THREE

Iowa, 1940

Juanita and Betty kept waiting for answers to their letters. They waited and waited. But they heard nothing from Anne and Margot and wondered why. Hardly any homes at that time had television, and unlike Margot and Anne, Betty and Juanita did not even have a radio. "In our house we didn't have electricity," Betty said. "It depended on if we could afford it." Frequently they used kerosene lamps for light.

To Betty and Juanita the war in Europe seemed far away from Iowa. They could only find out what was happening through magazines and newspapers. At the Danville Consolidated School, Miss Birdie kept her students informed about the war. On Fridays, "Current Events Day," she discussed newspaper articles and radio broadcasts. The *Des Moines Register* reported that the Iowa Quakers, or Friends, had fixed up the old Scattergood School in West Branch near Iowa City and had turned it into a hostel for European refugees of all faiths. The Friends planned on helping their "guests" learn English and adjust to a new life in America. One resident of the hostel later wrote that Scattergood was a "place of peace in a world of war, a haven amidst a world of hatred."

The *Danville Enterprise*, a weekly paper, had folded long before, but *The Daily Hawk-Eye Gazette*, published in Burlington, reported local as well as world news. On Friday, May 10, 1940, the headline read: *Allies aid Low countries as Hitler Starts "Total" War*. The lead article from Amsterdam told how Dutch and Belgian troops had fought hard against the Nazis. The front page carried an article quoting President Franklin D. Roosevelt. He said that although he sympathized with Queen Wilhelmina and her country, the United States would stay out of the war.

Juanita, age ten, and Betty, age fourteen

By Tuesday the headline proclaimed: *Holland Yields to Hitler*. A report from London told how the entire Dutch government had followed the royal family to England. *The Daily Hawk-Eye Gazette* printed a detailed "war map" of Holland, and its borders with France and Germany, to help readers understand the news. The Nazis were preparing to attack Great Britain from their new naval and air bases in Amsterdam and other Dutch cities.

Miss Birdie explained to her students that communications with Holland were now cut off. Betty and Juanita worried about Anne and Margot. "We wondered where our pen pals were, and how they were getting along during the repressive German occupation," Betty wrote. "Were bombs dropping nearby? What was it like to live in a war-torn

Ann and Elmer Wagner with baby Juanita and Betty, in front of their farmhouse

country?" The Wagner sisters still did not know that the Franks were Jewish and therefore subject to brutal treatment by the Nazis.

School ended in Danville at the end of May. The boys were needed on the farm to cultivate the crops. But on Betty and Juanita's eighty-acre farm, the girls helped with the work. When their father, Elmer, had become sick with Hodgkin's disease, their mother had taken charge. "The days of my dad's illness were hard for my mom, who was born and raised a city girl," recalled Betty. "Now she had to learn to milk a cow and feed the chickens and slop the pigs."

Elmer died in 1932, during the period known as the Great Depression. But he and his wife still owed money for the farm to

Grandpa Theodore Wagner and his three sisters, Iowa

Grandpa Wagner, whose land adjoined theirs. After the funeral family and friends gathered at Betty and Juanita's house. "Grandpa Wagner came in and told Mom that he wanted her to pay him what was owed him on the farm and machinery as soon as possible," recalled Betty, "and pointing and shaking his finger at her he said, 'Don't ever come to me for any help.'"

From that moment on, Betty, Juanita, and their mother were on their own. They rented their land to some farmers who raised the crops for them and then shared any money they earned with the Wagner family.

"As soon as Mom could she had a farm auction to sell everything and get cash to pay Grandpa Wagner," said Betty. During the school year, her mother taught at Possum Hollow, and the money she made had to last through the summer.

Possum Hollow schoolhouse

"Living on a farm, we always had milk and eggs and chickens," said Betty, "and in the summer we planted a big garden. I can remember how Mom, Juanita, and I tried to keep the weeds out of the garden, but by the middle of the summer they'd get ahead of us. We'd can all we could, including making our own catsup. . . . We also made a great green pimento and onion relish in the summer months. Juanita and I would sit outside by the pump on the platform and grind pimentos and onions by the hour as Mom stayed in and cooked it on the old kitchen range."

Betty's father had taught her how to mow hay and get it into the barn when she was just a little girl. "The hayloader was hooked to the back of the wagon, and one of us kids would carefully drive the horses down a row of raked hay," she recalled. "As the hay was raked and picked up into the hayloader and pulled to the top about ten feet, it was dropped onto the wagon. The real art of loading the hay wagon was to do it so perfectly that it would never tip over as you drove back to the barn to unload."

In spite of the hard work, the girls enjoyed treats. They swam in the creek and bicycled up to the creamery in Danville for an ice cream. Occasionally Betty and Juanita took interesting outings away from home.

Betty and cousin Jim Dunn on tractor pulling hay wagon, 1940

"During the summer months when Mom could afford the gas she would take us to see different kinds of factories and take the tours to learn how things were made and done," Betty remembered. "The button factory, the cookie factory—wherever it was free and had tours. Sometimes we went to Fort Madison to the penitentiary or Mt. Pleasant to the insane asylum." Their mother thought that these would be educational places for her girls to see.

Juanita and Betty with bikes in the front yard, 1941

Their cousin Fern often went with them. Fern lived "up the road" in New London, a nearby town. The only time Betty and Juanita ever saw movies was with Fern. Fern, like their Dutch pen pal Anne, bought movie magazines and collected pictures of stars. That spring a movie called *Everything Happens at Night* had played at the Zephyr Theater in Burlington. It featured Sonja Henie and Ray Milland, two of Anne's favorites.

"In the summer of 1940 we drove to Chicago for a couple of days of sightseeing," recalled Betty. "How exciting to see the tall buildings, to go to the zoo, and to ride the elevated trains. Juanita bought a small little Brownie Kodak camera at Marshall Field's for a dollar and I bought a compact."

That summer Betty had her first job away from home. Some neighbors a mile and a half away needed someone to help while their housekeeper was on vacation. "For $3.50 a week, for two weeks," she said, "I'd get up before daybreak, get dressed, ride my bicycle down to their house, go inside and start the kerosene stove, grind the coffee in their antique coffee grinder, and put the coffee pot on to boil. Then,

I'd go out and feed the chickens and milk the cow. . . . After breakfast I'd do the dishes. Then maybe we'd wash, using an old-fashioned wash-tub and scrubbing board with a handwringer, hanging the clothes out in the sun to dry. Or maybe I'd iron, or hoe in the garden or mow the lawn or dust or sweep, or whatever needed doing that day. Then make lunch and start over again until [it was] time to do milking and the evening chores and dinner and hope to get home before dark on my bicycle."

By September Betty and Juanita were more than ready to go back to school. The war still seemed distant, but in Iowa a peacetime draft was already in progress. President Roosevelt had ordered the governor of each state to draw up a list of people to head draft boards. Soldiers would have to be recruited if the United States entered the battle.

FOUR

Amsterdam, 1940–1941

"After May 1940," Anne wrote in her diary, "the good times were few and far between: first there was the war, then the capitulation and then the arrival of the Germans, which is when the trouble started for the Jews."

At night people were ordered to cover their windows with blackout paper. Air-raid sirens screamed. Anne and her friends cursed the German soldiers. Wearing their uniforms and metal helmets, they marched through Anne's neighborhood, which was called the River Quarter. "In the summer of 1940 we didn't do much for my birthday," Anne wrote, "since the fighting had just ended in Holland."

A girl named Eva who was Anne's age had recently moved into the River Quarter and lived on the other side of the park. Eva said, "During the invasion there were aeroplanes coming over from both sides. We were terrified by all the bombing and shooting. But with the surrender, things almost became normal again. We went back to our schools and it wasn't too bad for us Jewish people or anybody else."

Although Eva never knew Anne, she wanted to become her friend.

Anne, Sanne, and Hanneli formed a clique. "They were an inseparable trio," Eva recalled, "each of them a little more sophisticated than the rest of us—more like teenagers. . . ." The three friends would sit in the grassy park across the street from Anne's building and read fashion magazines, or discuss film stars and talk about boys.

That summer, when Anne was just eleven, she had her first romance with a fourteen-year-old boy named Peter. Later she wrote about it in her diary: "Peter crossed my path, and in my childish way I really fell in love. He also liked me very much and we couldn't be parted for one whole summer. I can still see us

Anne leans over the balcony of her apartment to watch a newlywed couple passing below, May 1941.

walking hand in hand through the streets together." But the romance ended when they went back to school. Peter's friends made fun of him for going around with a young girl who was only in the sixth grade.

In the fall Anne's teacher was Mrs. Kuperus, headmistress at Montessori. Either she or Anne's teacher the previous year, Miss Gadron, had set up the pen-pal program with Juanita's teacher, Miss Birdie. Anne adored Mrs. Kuperus but one of her classmates, Henny, did not. Henny remembered the teacher as "tall and stern."

"They called me strict but honest," said Mrs. Kuperus in an interview. "All children shook hands with Mrs. Kuperus morning and afternoon," said Henny, when they arrived at school and when they left. Henny sensed that she preferred children from well-to-do families like Anne's rather than from poorer families like hers.

Susanne (Sanne) Ledermann at school, around 1941

Henny's father was an artist but was able to sell few of his paintings. However, Montessori was open to all children and cost only fifty cents a day.

"We were terribly anxious about our school," Mrs. Kuperus recalled. "I had some problems with the Germans when they wanted to take the school for quarters for their soldiers, but I told them about the poor heating system and great amount of windows....When they saw we had no central heating they left again. Everything went on as before, and in fact the last year was particularly nice. We had started to do theatricals. The children wrote the plays in one class, and in the following class we put them on. Anne was in her element. Of course she was full of ideas for the scripts, but since she also had no shyness and liked imitating other people, the big parts fell to her. And in the middle of this lovely year came the decree."

The Nazis passed laws to separate Jews from the rest of the population. "A lot of laws were introduced in Holland, which made our lives harder," remembered Otto Frank. German Jews who had emigrated to Holland after 1933 were required to register with the Office for Resident Foreigners. Otto knew that Jews would soon have to give up their businesses. Therefore he transferred ownership of his company, Opekta, to trusted members of his staff: Victor Kugler and Johannes Kleiman, who were both non-Jews. And he appointed Miep's fiancé, Jan Gies, who now worked for him, as director of Pectacon, his spice company.

But the Nazis kept issuing new rules and regulations.

A curfew was imposed for everyone living in the Netherlands. No one could be out on the streets between midnight and four in the morning, and travel across the borders was forbidden. In November Jews were no longer allowed to work in government jobs or at universities. Books written by Jewish authors were banned and removed from schools and libraries. Jews were even afraid to keep these books at home in case they got searched by the police. Franz Ledermann, Sanne and Barbara's father, filled several big laundry baskets with books by forbidden authors on subjects such as philosophy, history, and politics, and burned them to protect his family.

In January 1941 Jews were forbidden to go to movie theaters. Because of Anne's love for movies, her father rented films and a projector and held private screenings in their apartment. Jewish musicians were not permitted to perform in orchestras paid for by the government. The Ledermanns and others played chamber music in their homes for invited friends and fellow music lovers. Jews were not allowed to eat in cafés and restaurants. By May the Nazis forbade Jews from swimming in public pools or visiting zoos and parks.

"We don't have much

Anne on the terrace of their apartment, 1940

33

Anne and her father, Otto Frank (in center), walking with other guests to the wedding of Miep and Jan Gies

chance to get tanned any more because we can't go to the swimming-pool," Anne wrote to "Omi," her grandmother in Switzerland. "It's a pity, but that's how it is." Instead, Anne and Margot sat on the terrace of their apartment to work on their tans.

The worst blow for Anne came at the end of the school year, just before her twelfth birthday. She, Hanneli, and their Jewish classmates had to fill out forms and register as Jews. Up till then, said Mrs. Kuperus, "There was no difference made between the Jewish and non-Jewish children. This began only when those dirty Germans started the war.

"We were a public school," she explained in an interview. "We received notice from the education department with a list of students who were not allowed to return to school after the summer vacation. We were ordered to give all the statistics of the Jewish children. There were eighty-seven of them in this school. We were forced to let eighty-seven pupils go. In Anne's class alone there were twenty.

"We informed them in small groups," said Mrs. Kuperus. "I remember that when we walked out of the hallway, I said good-bye to each individual."

Anne was stunned. Heartbroken. "I was in form 6B," she wrote, "when I had to say good-bye to Mrs. K. We both wept, it was very sad."

Nevertheless, the summer held some happy moments. On July 16, 1941, Miep married Jan Gies, whom she called Henk. Anne, dressed up in a light-colored coat and matching hat, attended the wedding with her father. Her mother had to stay home with Margot, who was sick, and Granny Holländer, who had just had an operation for cancer. Miep's wedding ceremony took place at City Hall. "Anne's eyes flicked nervously back and forth from Henk to me," Miep recalled. "She stayed close to her father, hanging on his hand. Perhaps we were the first romantic bride and groom she had ever seen in the flesh. A wedding was the number one romantic occasion for a girl of twelve." Afterward, Anne examined Miep's wedding band. "Anne was impressed with my gold ring," Miep said. "She looked at it dreamily. I'm sure she was imagining that someday she too would marry a tall, handsome man like Henk."

Miep and Jan Gies on their wedding day

The next morning Otto threw a small wedding party at his office at 263 Prinsengracht. "Anne wore a bright summer frock and was in a happy mood," Miep remembered. "She helped to lay out the meats on the plates, to cut the bread, to put out the butter. We all ate until we were stuffed. I was deeply touched by the presents that were given us. It was not easy to get nice things these days, but everyone had found a way. Anne presented me with a silver plate from the family and the office staff.

"I noticed how Anne kept her eyes on Henk and me; she was so enthralled by our romantic love story. She treated us almost as though we were two movie stars rather than two perfectly ordinary Dutch people who had simply married."

A few days later Anne went on vacation with Sanne Ledermann. "I'm in Beekbergen now," she wrote to Omi. Beekbergen was a country village where they stayed at a house that Sanne's relatives rented for the summer. "It's very nice here, but it's a pity the weather is so bad," wrote Anne. "The house is very old-fashioned but still pleasant. Sanne and I have our own little room. . . . I'm reading a lot. It's too bad we can't go outside."

When Anne wrote to her father she asked him to send more books. And in another letter she thanked him for sending money, which she spent on postcards, stamps, candy, and a notebook. Then she added,

Anne, Sanne, and Sanne's little cousin Ray, Beekbergen, Holland, 1941

"Many thanks for the two film-star cards, which came right after the first ones. I didn't have either one."

By September Anne and every Jew over the age of six had to carry an identity card displaying two photographs and stamped with a large black "J".

"Jews were forbidden to visit Christians in their homes," Anne wrote in her diary; "Jews were required to attend Jewish schools, etc. You couldn't do this and you couldn't do that, but life went on." Leaving old friends behind, she and Margot enrolled in their new school, the Jewish Lyceum.

FIVE

Iowa, 1941

Betty and Juanita did not realize that Anne and Margot were now at a different school. They kept hoping to hear from their pen pals. But no letters came.

In fall 1941 Betty went back to Danville Consolidated School, same as always. Now she was in eleventh grade. High-school classes met upstairs on the second floor, and lower grades were downstairs. That term there were more students than usual because of the ammunition plant that had been built in Middletown, just outside Danville.

At the plant workers loaded artillery shells and bombs for the War Department. "America's all-out defense effort," proclaimed *The Daily Hawk-Eye Gazette*.

Barbed-wire fencing surrounded the huge plant, which included manufacturing buildings, "storage igloos," and two fire stations in case of explosions. With the arrival of a construction crew, then factory workers, "Danville's population boomed . . . and brought many new families into town," recalled Doris Kelley, the wife of one of Juanita's classmates. "The school enrollment reflected this 'boom' and the

Juanita, age eleven, on the farm, 1941

classrooms were filled to overflowing."

"There were new kids at school," Betty remembered. "A lot of strangers came. Mom rented out the basement."

"Immediate housing was hard to find," wrote the town historians, "so plant workers found rooms in Danville, and many brought trailers. The streets of Danville became very conjested [sic] with these mobile homes." Some people even had to live in tents.

"The plant took thousands of acres of prime farm land," recalled Don Kellar, Miss Birdie's great nephew and student. But the plant brought sewer and water lines to Danville.

"We had running water for the first time," said Vivian Kellar, Don's wife, who lived in Middletown at that time. "Up 'till then everybody had an outhouse." Now there was indoor plumbing.

At Betty and Juanita's farm, they still used the outhouse, a "two-holer." The outhouse also had a little wooden toilet in the corner, twelve inches off the floor, that their father had built for the girls when they were small. "There was no such thing as toilet paper," Betty remembered. "We couldn't afford it." Instead they used pages from the Sears, Roebuck catalog and the one from Montgomery Ward.

That fall Juanita didn't return to school. "She missed Miss Birdie's seventh-grade class because of her eyes," said Betty. Juanita had some kind of infection and almost lost her vision. "We went to specialists in Marshalltown," Betty recalled. The doctors prescribed eyedrops and glasses. Although Juanita remained home alone each day, she kept up with her studies. Miss Birdie stayed in touch with the family and sent over assignments. Betty read books aloud to her sister. Their mother

Trailers purchased by the Federal Farm Security Administration to house ordnance plant workers, Burlington, Iowa, July 23, 1941

scraped together enough money to buy a little portable typewriter. Betty was taking typing as one of her high-school courses. "What I learned to do that day in typing," she said, "I came home and taught Juanita." Betty showed her sister what keys to press, and soon Juanita became an expert typist.

Meanwhile, their mother continued teaching at Possum Hollow. About once a month she attended meetings of country teachers at the Burlington Public Library. Betty and Juanita went with her, and Betty read newspapers and magazines to her sister.

The newspapers reported war bulletins: The Germans had marched into Paris, France, and had raised the Nazi flag on the Eiffel Tower. *Hitler Begins War on Russia*, read the headlines. Winston Churchill, prime minister of England, promised victory over the Germans. "Victory at all costs," he said. And President Roosevelt agreed to help the Allies. But he knew that Americans did not want to enter the war.

News began to leak out about Nazi atrocities. Eyewitnesses gave accounts that "Germany had set out to 'annihilate all the Jews in Europe.'" On May 18, 1941, *The New York Times* reported that German soldiers had gunned down more than 100,000 Jews in Poland and twice as many in western Russia. On June 1, 1941, the *Seattle Times* printed a front-page headline: *Jews Slain Total 200,000!*

In Pittsburgh, Pennsylvania, a group offered a $1 million cash reward for the capture of Adolf Hitler "alive, unwounded and unhurt." They wanted to bring the German dictator to trial before a world court of "civilized nations." At the same time, however, feelings of antisemitism ran high in the United States. Jewish leaders tried unsuccessfully to convince President Roosevelt to let more immigrants into the U.S. and thus save European Jews. As early as 1939, Catholic and Protestant clergymen had petitioned the White House at least to bring in German children, half of whom were not Jewish. A bill proposing that ten thousand children be admitted that year, and another ten thousand the

Artists in the Work Projects Administration's (WPA) Iowa Art program created this propaganda poster to symbolize armed forces and industry working together to crush Hitler.

next year, was introduced in Congress. The American Friends Service Committee offered to supervise all the arrangements. Even the president's wife, Eleanor Roosevelt, vigorously supported the bill. But the president did nothing because of the political climate.

Many Americans were prejudiced against Jews and feared that foreigners would take away their jobs. "Are we to harbor all the riff raff of Europe?" wrote an angry citizen to his congressman. "The Jews take over everything here." The fact that America was considered "the melting pot," a land of immigrants, seemed to have been forgotten.

Betty and Juanita's own grandparents had emigrated from Europe. On their mother's side Grandpa Dunn had come from Scotland, and Grandma Dunn had left Ireland in 1880 after the terrible years of the potato famine, when Irish people still remembered and feared starvation. Their dad's parents, the Wagners, had come from Düsseldorf, Germany. For the first time Betty felt uncomfortable about "her good German name," Wagner. Betty and Juanita wondered what was happening to Anne and Margot under German rule. "We often talked about the Franks," Betty recalled. "Were they alive? Were they safe?"

That winter, for the first time, Betty and Juanita had electricity at their house *and* a radio! It was "a big old console that sat on the floor like a piece of furniture," Betty recalled. One Sunday in December, they were listening to the *Old Fashioned Revival Hour* with some friends who had come over from Burlington for a visit. All of a sudden an announcer interrupted the program and said that the Japanese had bombed Pearl Harbor. Everyone gathered around the radio. "We didn't even know where Pearl Harbor was," said Betty. "We were very surprised." The next day President Roosevelt asked Congress to declare war on Japan. He spoke to the nation over the radio and began, "Yesterday, December 7, 1941—a date that will live in infamy—the United States of America was suddenly and deliberately attacked by naval and air forces of the Empire of Japan. The United States was at peace with that nation...."

A few days later Hitler declared war on the United States. By Friday, December 12, the United States was at war with Germany and Italy, Japan's Axis partners.

In Danville, draft notices began arriving. "So many young men were called up," remembered Dan Kelley, Juanita's classmate. In the school paper, *The Danvillian*, Juanita and Betty could read the reports:

"Sherman Walker enlisted in the mechanics division of the Air Corps."

"Dale Murry is stationed at Shepherd's Field, Texas."

"Wendell Mathews left for the army, Thursday." (He was another one of Miss Birdie's nephews.)

In the spring, Betty's physics

WW II political cartoon relating to Pearl Harbor

teacher enlisted in the air force and became a bombardier.

Mr. Orndorff, superintendent of the school, was in his mid-forties at that time and too old to go into service. So he printed a "Notice to All Farmers!!" It read: "Mr. Orndorff, being patriotic minded, will be only too happy to help out on the farms on Saturdays and after school hours on school days. He feels that this is his patriotic duty."

Harold Griffith with some of the hogs raised as part of the "Food-for-Victory" program. (Nine miles east of) Audubon, Iowa, September 1942

"Pearl Harbor... triggered the patriotism in the people because they were just so incensed about it," remembered another Iowan, Ida Belle Sands, of Terril, whose husband was stationed on Okinawa, an island in the Pacific Ocean. "They were willing to do anything—anything at all—to win the war . . . Everybody . . . pitched in. In fact, they were a slacker if they didn't. People's houses had yellow paint dumped on them sometimes . . . the color yellow just represented 'slacker.' Not too many people had that done to them. Everybody just pitched in."

Two years after the Nazis invaded Poland, and one year after they invaded Holland, the United States—and Iowa—entered the war. Like Margot and Anne, Betty and Juanita felt for the first time the realities of the present world situation. But unlike Margot and Anne, they did not witness battles that were fought in their very own yard.

SIX

Amsterdam, September 1941–July 1942

Unbeknownst to Juanita and Betty, their pen pals had started going to a new school, a lycée. In October 1941, when Anne was twelve and Margot was fifteen, they began attending classes at the Jewish Lyceum. Anne's old friend Hanneli and Margot's best friend, Jetteke, went there, too. Sanne went to a different lycée, and her sister, Barbara, who loved to dance, enrolled at a Jewish-owned ballet school.

At first Anne didn't like her new school because she and Hanneli were put in different classes. "I hadn't discovered a single person I knew who would become a class-mate, and that situation didn't strike me as very pleasant," she later wrote in a story, "My First Day at the Lyceum." "When I was given the desk at the very back of the class, behind girls much bigger than myself, I felt lonely and forsaken." So Anne asked her gym teacher to have Hanneli transferred to her class.

At the end of the first school day, Anne bicycled home and on her way met a new friend, Jacqueline van Maarsen. Jacque (pronounced "Jackie") also lived in the River Quarter. "She [Anne] was in my class at school," recalled Jacque years later in her book, *My Friend Anne Frank*.

"I hadn't noticed her there that morning and had to ask her name. 'Anne Frank,' she said. She took me home with her, introduced me at once to her mother and sister as her new school friend, and went to feed her black cat already circling her, mewing and rubbing its head against her. Then her grandmother, who lived with them, had to meet me, and I met Anne's father that day, too, because Anne said after an hour, when I wanted to call home, 'Just say you'll be staying for dinner.' Anne talked endlessly, telling me all about her girlfriends and her previous school, and wanted to

Anne during the school year, 1941–1942

know everything about me. Both of us had attended a Montessori school.

"It was very cozy and pleasant at Anne's house," wrote Jacque, "and I felt immediately at home. When Mr. Frank returned home later, he

took the time to talk with me extensively. I told him that I had to go to Jewish High School instead of Girls High School even though I didn't have a Jewish mother and why."

Jacque's mother had come from France and had been raised a Catholic. However, when she fell in love with Jacque's father, a Jew, she converted to Judaism before they married. Then they moved from Paris to Amsterdam. Jacque's mother worked in a fashionable department store, and her father traded in old books and prints.

Jacque, around 1943

Dit is een foto, zoals
ik me zou wensen,
altijd zo te zijn.
Dan had ik nog wel
een kans om naar
Holywood te komen.
Anne Frank.
10 Oct. 1942

(translation)
"This is a photo as I would wish
myself to look all the time. Then
I would maybe have a chance to
come to Hollywood."
Anne Frank, 10 Oct. 1942

Photograph of Anne, 1939, which she placed in her diary on October 10, 1942

"After a couple of days," Jacque wrote, "Anne declared that I was her best friend and she was mine." Like Anne, Jacque adored movies and collected postcards of American film stars. "My movie star collection was much smaller than Anne's," Jacque wrote. However, her entire collection of cards was bigger. "My only idols were Deanna Durbin and Shirley Temple." Anne had a Shirley Temple card that had been sent to her sister, Margot. Anne still dreamed of going to Hollywood. Perhaps she imagined meeting her pen pals in Iowa along the way. On a picture of herself taken that year, she wrote, "This is a photo as I would wish myself to look all the time. Then I would maybe have a chance to go to Holywood [sic]."

"We traded cards," said Jacque, "and since my collection was larger I also gave her some of my cards that she especially liked." The ones Anne wanted were cards of the little English princesses that Jacque had bought on a trip to Paris with her mother.

Anne and Jacque shared many interests. They both loved to play Monopoly, and they read the same books. Jacque owned a copy of *The Myths of Greece and Rome*, and Anne loved the illustrations. She wanted a copy for her birthday. The girls particularly enjoyed novels by Cissy van Marxveldt that had been written for teenagers. Their favorite was a series about an adventurous young woman named Joop. "We especially liked the one with romance," recalled Jacque, "the one where she meets her future husband." In the story Joop has a best friend named Kitty, and she writes to pen pals, just as Anne had done. Anne's father had helped her and Margot with their letters to Betty and Juanita by translating them into English. But Joop's father forbids her to write any more letters, so she begins to keep a diary. Anne and Jacque read passages from the books to each other and acted out scenes.

They even did their homework together at Anne's house. Jacque remembered the kitchen at Anne's, "the kitchen where Anne always stood making sandwiches after school at four o'clock and where she fed her cat, Moortje." When the weather was nice, the girls climbed out the window onto the terrace and read and talked, sitting in deck chairs. "We told each other all kinds of secrets there," said Jacque.

A big topic of conversation was boys. Anne was curious about sexual relations between men and women. Her mother refused to discuss the subject, and her father only told her a few bits of information. "I was able to enlighten her somewhat," Jacque wrote, "since my sister had already told me the essentials a few years earlier."

Jacque and Anne liked to play Ping-Pong and started a club. "Another girl, Ilse, had a Ping-Pong table at home," Jacque wrote. "We

Cover of *Joop ter Heul*, a book written as a series of letters

often went there to play. We formed the Ping-Pong club because there was so little we were allowed to do."

The club was called "'the Little Dipper Minus Two,'" Anne wrote in her diary. "A really silly name, but it's based on a mistake. We wanted to give our club a special name; and because there were five of us, we came up with the idea of the Little Dipper. We thought it consisted of five stars, but we turned out to be wrong. It has seven, like the big Dipper, which explains the 'Minus Two.'

"Susanne Ledermann is our president, Jacqueline van Maarsen the secretary, Elisabeth [Hanneli] Goslar, Ilse and I are the other members . . . Our games usually end with a visit to the nearest ice cream parlor that allows Jews," Anne wrote, "either Oasis or Delphi." The girls never sat inside. They bought their ice-cream and went outside to socialize. "We always ran into people we knew there," recalled Jacque. "Anne loved walking behind boys and fantasizing that they were all her admirers. I didn't notice too much admiring going on, but they probably found her amusing, since she was cheerful and lively."

Sometimes Anne and Jacque slept over at each other's house. When Anne came to Jacque's, she brought along a suitcase and "a cosmetic case with her curlers, hairbrush, and cape," recalled Jacque's mother.

While Anne and Margot continued going to school and spending time with friends, their parents tried to keep them from worrying too much about what was happening all around them. "Naturally the children knew what was going on," Otto wrote. "After all, they had been forced to change schools, and they could not help hearing the military cars in the streets at night." Without warning, the Nazis rounded up Jews and took them away. In a letter to her uncle, Sanne wrote, "Today I skipped school because of possible raids." Rumors spread that soon all the Jews in Holland would be deported. Otto wrote to his relatives in Switzerland, "Day by day, life is getting harder."

He tried to make arrangements for his family to emigrate to the United States by first going to a neutral country—Cuba, Portugal, or Spain. To do this, he needed a sponsor in the United States. So Otto wrote to his wife's brothers, Julius and Walter Holländer, who lived in Leominster, Massachusetts, and asked if his family could live with them when they arrived. Of course Julius and Walter said yes. Then Julius contacted Otto's old friend Nathan Straus, Jr. in New York and asked him to help pay for the Franks' transportation. Julius assured Straus that he and his brother "will do all we can to refund your expenses." They probably hoped that Straus would have influence with government officials. Straus had been appointed as head of the United States Housing Authority in 1937 by President Roosevelt and was still serving in that capacity. But the most important part of the plan was obtaining permission for the Franks to leave Holland.

A letter to Julius dated November 1941, from the National Refugee Service in New York, stated: "We have been recently informed that persons in occupied areas are being denied exit permits. It may be that even after the Franks have obtained Cuban visas they may fail to obtain the necessary exit permits from Holland."

Next, Otto tried to take his family to England, where his older brother, Robert, had lived since 1933. On January 20, 1942, the Franks applied to the Central Office for Emigration for permission to leave. But their application was "postponed indefinitely."

In the meantime, Granny Holländer's health grew worse, and at the end of January she died of cancer. Anne and Margot were grief-stricken. Anne later wrote in her diary, "No one knows how often *I* think of her and still love her."

The situation in Holland became increasingly dangerous as the Nazis stepped up persecution of the Jews. They arrested Jews trying to leave Holland illegally. And they arrested non-Jews who helped them. In April 1942 all Jews over the age of six were required to wear yellow cloth stars printed with the word *JOOD* ("Jew") in black. Jews even had to wear the stars in their own gardens, or on their balconies, or at the doors and windows of their homes.

Nevertheless, Anne happily celebrated her thirteenth birthday on Friday, June 12, 1942. One of her gifts was a diary. She had chosen it herself at a neighborhood store that sold books and stationery. The

Students from the Jewish school on Cliffordstraat, a street in Amsterdam, 1942

diary was covered in red-and-white plaid. That morning, when her friend Hanneli came to pick her up for school, Anne showed her the diary before they left. They had to walk a long way because a few days earlier the Nazis had forbidden Jews to use public transportation. In the past the girls had often taken the tram to school when they didn't ride their bikes.

That afternoon Hanneli, Jacque, Sanne, and Ilse came over to Anne's house and gave her a joint birthday present, a book called *Dutch Sagas and Legends*. The girls also came to Anne's birthday party on Sunday. Other guests included Margot and her friend Jetteke, and some of Anne's classmates. Since Jews were not permitted to go to public theaters, Anne's father rented a projector and showed one of Anne's favorite American movies, *Rin-Tin-Tin and the Lighthouse Keeper*. Her mother served homemade strawberry tart and milk. The next day Anne wrote in her diary, "The Rin Tin Tin movie was a big hit."

Less than two weeks later, on June 22, Jews were ordered to turn in their bicycles to the Nazis. The Franks refused to obey this command. "Daddy has given Mummy's to some Christian acquaintances for safe-keeping," Anne wrote in her diary. Her own bicycle had been stolen during Easter vacation. But the Franks secretly held on to Margot's in case they needed it.

Around this time Otto told Anne and Margot that the family might have to go into hiding. "But when, Father?" asked Anne as they took a walk.

"Don't you worry," he said. "We'll take care of everything. Just enjoy your carefree life while you can."

Anne had just met a sixteen-year-old boy named Hello Silberberg, and she greatly enjoyed his attention. "He's just a friend," she wrote, "or as Mother puts it, a beau."

On Sunday, July 5, after a visit from Hello, Anne was sitting outside on the terrace reading when the doorbell rang. A policeman delivered a call-up notice. The family panicked. At first they thought the notice was for Otto. "A call-up," Anne wrote, "everyone knows what that means. Visions of concentration camps and lonely cells race through my head." But the notice turned out to be for Margot, who was sixteen. The Nazis were rounding up thousands of boys and girls, sixteen and older, and told them they were sending them to work camps in Germany. Most went without protesting. Very few refused to go because they thought their families would be endangered if they said no. Before Sanne's older sister, Barbara, was called up, she decided with some friends to go underground. Barbara had warnings about what was really happening in the so-called German "workcamps." She took off her star and, with her blond hair, assumed a new identity.

The Franks immediately decided to go into hiding the next day. "Margot and I started packing our most important belongings into a schoolbag," Anne wrote. "The first thing I stuck in was this diary, and then curlers, handkerchiefs, schoolbooks, a comb and some old letters."

Were the "old letters" from her pen pals in Iowa?

SEVEN

Iowa, 1942–1943

In Danville school began on August 31, 1942. Juanita had recovered from her eye infection and entered ninth grade. Betty was in her senior year of high school. The sisters had no idea that their Dutch pen pals had fled from their home and were keeping up with *their* studies while in hiding.

American newspapers told little if anything about the Nazis' persecution of the Jews in Europe. When the archbishop of Westminster made a special broadcast from England stating that the Nazis had massacred seven hundred thousand Jews in Poland, people said, "Oh! British propaganda!" But the American State Department began looking into the situation and confirmed the reports. A mass demonstration protesting Nazi atrocities was held in New York City on July 21, 1942. President Roosevelt sent a message of support, and so did Prime Minister Churchill, who said over the radio that "the Jews were Hitler's first victims." Jewish leaders called upon European countries to take notice of the tragedy and bring the Nazis to justice.

Betty and Juanita still did not know that Anne and Margot were

Juanita, age twelve, November 1942

Jewish. "You grow up on a small farm in Iowa," Betty said, "and you don't know a Jewish person from any other person."

Betty and Juanita remained safe in Iowa, far away from the public outcry and fighting. "In the middle of the country like that you feel safe," said Betty. "Like all Americans, we were never afraid." Of course, many children prayed that Hitler would never come over to the United States.

In churches and synagogues throughout the country prayers were offered for friends and family members fighting overseas. "Our little church offered prayers, especially in morning and evening services," Betty recalled, "and at mid-week prayer meetings after supper."

Betty worried about her classmates who had enlisted or were drafted. "Some of the kids I went to school with went off to war," she recalled. "Most of the guys went to fight. Some went to the Pacific, some to Europe. There were only sixteen of us in the graduating class." The previous year there had been twenty-one.

"After graduation practically everyone went into service," remembered Dan Kelley, Juanita's classmate.

Betty, a typist for the

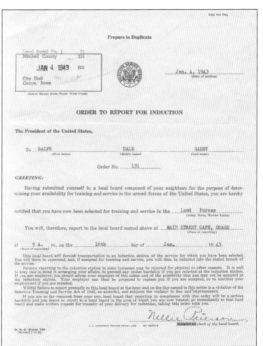

1943 draft induction order

school paper, *The Danvillian*, printed reports about all the members of the community who were in the armed services:

"Russel Williams left for Nashville, Tenn. Sept. 1. He is in the Air Corps."

"Dwight Rice, of the U.S. Navy in Norfolk, Virginia, is home visiting his father, A. G. Rice of Danville."

An editorial in the September issue read: "The staff of the DANVILLIAN is busy working on the high school paper. Numerous plans are being completed to make it a better paper this year in spite of the problems that the war causes it to face."

In Iowa, as in the rest of the United States, there was a shortage of gas, food, and metal. Consumers had to return used toothpaste tubes, for example, in order to buy new ones. "Your toothpaste tubes were metal," explained Ida Belle Sands of Terril. "The merchant when he had so many would turn those in. That was used for steel."

The government issued ration stamps for purchasing many things,

Cartoon related to rationing scrap metal

from coffee and sugar to gasoline. "The biggest problem was no gasoline," recalled Betty. "We had to live on ration stamps for meat. We had chicken and eggs if all else failed."

In the summer Betty, Juanita, and their mother raised vegetables in a "great big garden," Betty remembered. "We canned everything, all the vegetables we could: tomatoes, peas, green beans." In the fall they even canned "cold pack beef" and made jelly from the grapes that grew in their arbor.

Iowa farmers pledged to supply enough food for American soldiers and sailors and the Allies by growing "victory gardens." Their motto was "Food for freedom."

Dorothy Moeller of Waverly recalled how the green-bean crop was ready to be picked, but most of the workforce was away in the armed services. "So we got together and decided that we had to do something," she said. "The whole town closed up that day and we all went out and we picked beans. We picked beans all day and we saved the crop. And of course, food was like gold, food was ammunition because it was needed for the war effort."

There were slogans such as "Bacon is a bullet against Hitler," "American farmers are fighting the good fight," and "In this war victory begins on the farm."

Elaine Finke, editor of *The Danvillian* wrote, "When we are told by the clerks in the stores that certain articles are not available, it is not because the clerk does not like us. It is because our men on the front lines need it worse than we do."

Page from Anna Wilson's scrapbook, "Schools at War," a class project for fourth grade, Garfield School, Ottumwa, Iowa, 1942–1945

"The grocers collected the stamps," recalled Dan Kelley, Juanita's classmate. "They were really strict about it."

In another editorial Elaine commented on gas rationing: "We must curtail our unnecessary driving. Does a pleasure jaunt to a movie on Saturday night seem more important than winning the war?"

"Farmers got more gas for their tractors," said Dan. An ad in the school paper read: "Keep your car in good condition if you want it to last for the duration by bringing it to Albright Garage." Tires could not be replaced because there was a shortage of rubber.

Many students, Betty and Juanita among them, helped with the war effort by planting victory gardens, rolling bandages to send overseas, and purchasing War bonds.

WPA gardeners harvesting green-bean crop for local school lunch program, Dows, Iowa, 1940

"I remember getting out of school going on a scrap metal drive," said Dan. "Probably 12 or 13 of us went out. We would load up trucks [with scrap metal], bring it into town, and ship it out."

The farm boys also pitched in for the harvest. "We were out there picking corn," said Dan,

"Mrs. Marquardt and her daughter, Vera, canned lots of food this year so that they may further restrict their canned goods purchases in 1943. Their only difficulty is their onions. They haven't yet found a way to keep them from sprouting." Location: probably Des Moines, Iowa

"because so many young men had been called up."

Juanita and Betty, and their class-mates at Danville School, kept up with some of the war news through movies. In the auditorium they watched *Movietone News* newsreel clips and films such as *Spotting the Bomber*, *London Fire Raids*, and *A Letter from Bataan*. But none of them really knew anything about Hitler's plan to deport or murder every Jew in Europe. They did not realize that in Holland, Hitler had driven the Frank family and thousands of Jews into hiding.

"We were very ignorant of all that," said Betty. "I don't remember hearing about the Holocaust." But the word *holocaust*, derived from the Greek word *holokauston* and meaning "an offering consumed by fire," had not yet come into usage when referring to the mass extermination of the Jews.

Meanwhile, more and more young men from Danville shipped out to fight in the war. "The boyfriend of a girl in my class was flying over Germany," recalled Betty. News came that he had been captured as a prisoner of war. But Betty's friend never lost hope. She knew that her boyfriend would come back, and eventually he did.

Others did not make it home.

"One day when we were in science class," remembered Dan, "Russel Williams's father came to school. He took Russel's sister Naomi out of class and told her that Russel had been killed over in Europe." Iowans placed stars in their windows: blue for

Photograph taken from Fox *Movietone News* newsreel

members of the family in the armed services, and gold for those missing in action or killed.

The largest number per capita of American prisoners of war (POWs) from any state came from Iowa. Thearl Mesecher of Des Moines kept a diary describing his day-to-day experiences as a POW in Germany. "Here we live two hundred and fifty men in one barracks, beds only two feet apart and two decks," he wrote. "Being a prisoner of war is about the worst predicament that one could possibly get into."

By 1942 the War Department started sending thousands of German prisoners to the United States. Prisoner-of-war camps needed to be far from the Canadian and Mexican borders so that the inmates could not escape into another country. And the camps could not be close to big cities, shipyards, or airplane factories. So two camps were built on the Iowa prairie in 1943. One was in the town of Clarinda and the other in Algona. The prisoners worked as cooks, bakers, cabinetmakers, sign painters, and gardeners. At Christmas some made toys for the children of their guards. A number of POWs had fond memories of their time in captivity because of their good relationship with the community.

"All Iowa officers' group," POWs in Nazi-occupied Poland, 1943

However, Juanita and Betty, like many young people in Iowa, did not realize how close the war had come to them.

Meanwhile, Californians urged their congressmen and President Roosevelt to round up and imprison Japanese-Americans. After the sneak attack on Pearl Harbor, they feared that these "persons of Japanese ancestry" would be more loyal to Japan than to America during the war. So President Roosevelt issued Executive Order 9066 and on March 18, 1942, signed Executive Order 9102. These laws, a disgrace to the United States, gave the government authority to evacuate more than 110,000 people of Japanese parentage from their homes

Manzanar War Relocation Camp in California (above) was the first of ten War Relocation Centers for Japanese Americans in the United States, including one in Tule Lake, California (below).

and send them to "Relocation Centers." The internment camps, surrounded by barbed wire, were located in desolate sections of California, Arizona, Utah, Arkansas, Idaho, Wyoming, and Colorado. Five hundred Japanese Americans were "resettled" in Des Moines, Iowa, yet many Japanese-American brothers, husbands, or sons of those interned loyally served in the armed services. Hysteria had spread in Iowa, too, and people felt prejudiced against Japanese Americans. Although they desperately needed help on the farm, many Iowans felt reluctant to hire these newcomers. "I wouldn't have one on the place!" declared one farm wife.

News of the internment camps reached Danville. "We didn't know who to trust," recalled Betty. Just as she had never known any Jews, she did not know any Japanese Americans. In spring 1943 she graduated from Danville School. The school picnic, usually held at the end of the year, was canceled. "Because of the war we must give up some pleasures," read the editorial in *The Danvillian*. "This year the senior class gave up their senior trip because of this problem. Also the music contests and other contests were given up.

"Everyone should do his part and do without some forms of recreation which are a waste of vital war materials."

Within a few days after graduation, Betty and three of her girlfriends left Danville. "We rode a coach train all the way to Washington, D.C., to work for the F.B.I.," she wrote. The FBI (Federal Bureau of

Investigation) had sent information to Danville School earlier in the year in order to recruit students. "Mr. Orndorff [the superintendent] had told me about it," said Betty. "He knew I was interested. I did a paper on the F.B.I. G-Men always intrigued me." *G-men* stands for "government men," the

J. Edgar Hoover at desk with "G-Men"

nickname for FBI agents. Newspaper and magazine articles celebrated their exploits as they tracked down and captured criminals.

Betty and her friends filled out applications, had their backgrounds checked, and were accepted. "While I was in Washington, Mom and Juanita moved from the farm to Burlington," Betty recalled. "They rented a small apartment on South Central. Mom had gotten a job in a machine shop and Juanita had lied about her age and was waitressing." The Wagners rented their Danville farm to a neighbor.

Despite the changes in their lives, Betty and Juanita kept thinking about the Franks. "We talked about them as we heard news over the

radio or saw something in the newspaper," recalled Betty. "We wondered if they were anywhere near where bombs were dropping." Betty and Juanita did not write any more letters to Anne and Margot for fear of causing trouble. "And when the war started we didn't plan on hearing from them," said Betty. Yet, if Anne and Margot *did* send mail, they would surely receive it. "Everyone knew where we were," said Betty.

Betty graduating from high school, 1943

EIGHT

Amsterdam, 1942

Early on a rainy Monday morning, July 6, 1942, Anne, Margot, and their parents hurriedly left their apartment. No one knew where they were going except for Otto's trusted staff. Otto had just written to his mother in Switzerland hinting that they would be in hiding. "Please don't be in any way concerned, if you hear little from us," he wrote. And he sent a similar letter to Edith's brothers, Julius and Walter, in Massachusetts, in care of his mother.

In a note for their lodger, Mr. Goldschmidt, who had rented a room from them, Otto suggested that they had gone to Switzerland. And Edith purposely scribbled the address of a German officer Otto had known and left it behind to give the impression that they were going to get help in escaping Holland.

Anne and Margot never had a chance to say good-bye to their friends. "At seven-thirty we closed the door behind us," Anne wrote in her diary. "Moortje, my cat, was the only living creature I said good-bye to. According to a note we left for Mr. Goldschmidt, she was to be taken to the neighbors, who would give her a good home."

The back of the secret annex (tall center building) at 263 Prinsengracht, photographed just after the war. Anne's room is at left half concealed by curtain.

The Franks wore as many clothes as they could despite the warm rain. "The four of us were wrapped in so many layers of clothes, it looked as if we were going off to spend the night in a refrigerator," Anne wrote. "No Jew in our situation would dare leave the house with a suitcase full of clothes."

Margot removed her yellow star and went ahead on her bicycle with Miep. "We pedaled evenly, not too fast," recalled Miep, "in order to appear like two everyday working girls on their way to work on Monday morning."

Anne and her parents, carrying shopping bags, walked in the pouring rain. On the way Otto and Edith told Anne where they were going, and how they had been sending furniture and belongings in advance. "The hiding place was located in Father's office building," Anne wrote. "Father didn't have a lot of people working in his office, just Mr. Kugler, Mr. Kleiman, Miep and a twenty-three year old typist named Bep Voskuijl, all of whom were informed of our coming." When the

Otto Frank and his staff. From left to right: Miep Gies, Johannes Kleiman, Otto Frank, Victor Kugler, and Bep Voskuijl

Franks reached 263 Prinsengracht they climbed a steep staircase to the third floor. Anne described the layout: "At the top of the stairs is a landing with doors on either side. The door to the right of the landing leads to the 'Secret Annex' at the back of the house. No one would ever suspect there were so many rooms behind that plain gray door." Anne and Margot shared one room, and their parents another. There were two more rooms for friends who would soon be joining them, Mr. and Mrs. van Pels and their son, Peter, and upstairs a living room and cooking area for everyone.

"Our living room and all the other rooms were so full of stuff that I can't find the words to describe it," Anne wrote. "All the cardboard boxes that had been sent to the office in the last few months were piled on the floors and beds . . . If we wanted to sleep in properly made beds that night, we had to get going and straighten up the mess. Mother and Margot were unable to move a muscle. They lay down on their bare mattresses, tired, miserable and I don't know what else. But Father and I, the two cleaner-uppers in the family, started in right away."

Next, Anne and her father sewed curtains out of "loose strips of material" and tacked them up to completely cover the windows. Everyone in Holland was ordered to cover their windows with blackout curtains at night, but the Franks didn't want anyone to catch sight of them during the day as well.

By the end of the week, Anne had fixed up the bedroom she shared with Margot. "Thanks to Father—who brought my entire postcard and movie-star collection here beforehand," she wrote, "—and to a brush and a pot of glue, I was able to plaster the walls with pictures. It looks much more cheerful." The pictures Anne put up above her desk and bed included clippings of American movie stars Priscilla and Rosemary Lane, who were sisters; Ginger Rogers; and Norma Shearer.

Yet Anne wrote, "I don't think I'll ever feel at home in this house, but that doesn't mean I hate it. It's more like being on vacation in some strange pension. . . . The Annex is an ideal place to hide in."

The hardest part for Anne was the silence. Otto told them the rules: In daytime they must remain quiet so that no one downstairs, other than their trusted helpers, would suspect they were there. They could not even use the toilet in the bathroom until night. "Father and I improvised a chamber pot, sacrificing a canning jar for this purpose," Anne wrote. "As far as I was concerned, this wasn't half as difficult as having to sit still all day and not say a word." Anne felt better when she heard the church bells chiming next door. "Daddy, Mummy, and Margot can't get used to the sound of the Westertoren clock yet, which tells us the time every quarter of an hour. I can. I loved it from the start, and especially in the night it's like a faithful friend."

Anne hated staying cooped up indoors. "Of course we can't ever look out the window or go outside," she wrote when they first arrived. And later she added, "Not being able to go outside upsets me more than I can say." Longingly she peeked out her window at the three-hundred-year old chestnut tree in a neighbor's garden. "There's always a tiny black cat roaming around the yard," she wrote, "and it reminds me of my dear sweet Moortje.

"Moortje is my weak spot. I miss her every minute of the day, and no one knows how often I think of her; whenever I do, my eyes fill with tears. Moortje is so sweet, and I love her so much that I keep dreaming she'll come back to us." The first time Miep came up to the hiding place to get the Franks' shopping list, Anne fired questions at her. "What about Moortje? Have you seen my cat? Is the lodger caring for her or has he given her away? What about my friends . . . who's there?

Have any of them gone into hiding like us?"

Miep told Anne that she had not seen Moortje, but she had seen Jacque's mother, and they were still living in their apartment. "Anne's face darkened," Miep recalled. "She wanted more news of her friends, she so missed her friends."

Otto had anticipated this problem. "From the start it was clear to us that a life in total seclusion would be much harder for the lively Anne to put up with than for us," he wrote. "We knew that she would miss greatly her many friends and school. Margot, who was more mature, would come to terms with our situation."

To keep the girls busy, Otto organized a routine of chores, studies, and reading for pleasure. "Above all the children had to have enough books to read and to learn," he wrote. "None of us wanted to think how long this voluntary imprisonment would last." Anne and Margot

Anne's room in the secret annex was temporarily refurnished for shooting a film.

continued their regular lessons. They both kept diaries and agreed to let each other read certain parts. Anne wrote hers as letters addressed to "Kitty," the character in the book series by Cissy van Marxveldt that she had shared with Jacque. She couldn't, of course, write to her real pen pal in Iowa or her friends in Amsterdam. "Who else but me is ever going to read these letters?" she wrote. But in her diary she composed a farewell letter to Jacque anyway. "I hope we'll meet again soon, but it probably won't be before the end of the war," she wrote, and signed it, "Your *'best'* friend Anne." "P.S.," she added, "I hope that we'll always stay *'best'* friends until we meet again."

Anne knew that she couldn't send the letter but pretended that she had and the same day had received an answer. "Dear Jackie," she wrote, "I was very glad to get your letter. I forgot to tell you in my last letter that you must not keep these letters from me, because no one must find them. So cut them up into tiny pieces."

"The diary was a constant companion for Anne," recalled Miep, "and also a source of teasing by the others. How was she finding so much to write about? Anne blushed when she was teased but to be safe, she kept her diary in her father's old leather briefcase."

At night Otto read aloud to his family, or they played board games. And when no one was in the office, they all went downstairs to listen to classical music and news over the wireless (radio). "Through the wireless we could feel connected to the outside world," Otto wrote. The news troubled them. Broadcasts from England reported that Jews were being killed by machine guns, grenades, and even poisoned by gas. When Miep came up for her daily visit, she told them what was happening in Amsterdam. "Our many Jewish friends and acquaintances are being taken away in droves," Anne wrote. "The Gestapo is treating them very roughly and transporting them in cattle cars to Westerbork, the big camp in Drenthe to which they're sending all the Jews.

"If it's that bad in Holland, what must it be like in those faraway and uncivilized places where the Germans are sending them? . . . There are no greater enemies on earth than the Germans and the Jews," Anne concluded.

In another entry she wrote, "I'm terrified our hiding place will be discovered and that we'll be shot."

Nevertheless the Franks hung onto their belief that the war would end and they would be able to come out of hiding. In the meantime Otto's staff took care of them. "Mr. Kugler sold spices without booking sales to help finance our needs," Otto recalled. "Miep and Bep had the extremely difficult task to provide food. They had to buy in different shops, so that it would not raise suspicion if they bought big quantities in one." Miep later said that she enjoyed the challenge. "I would go to all the shops," she recalled, "and you would try things out a little with the man in the shop. How far you could go. How much you could ask." Bep set aside bottles of milk intended for the office staff.

Mr. Kleiman had a friend who owned a bakery, and he supplied the family with bread. "Bread is delivered twice daily," Anne wrote. "Of course, we don't have as much as we did at home, but it's enough. We also purchase ration books on the black market" (illegally). Just like Betty and Juanita in America, they could buy goods only with ration stamps issued by the government. Miep's husband, Jan Gies, was able to purchase ration cards for the Franks through his work in a Resistance group, the National Relief Fund.

Each week Kugler managed to bring Anne copies of her favorite movie magazine, *Cinema & Theater*. And Bep told Anne all about the movies she saw. Anne wrote, "Moms recently remarked that I wouldn't need to go to the movies later on because I already know the plots, the names of the stars and the reviews by heart."

"Sometimes Anne would spread out her movie-star photo collection to look at and admire the glamorous faces," Miep recalled. "She'd talk about movies and movie stars with anyone who would listen."

Otto wrote in his memoir: "Nobody could imagine what it meant for us that my four employees proved to be sacrificial helpers and genuine friends, in a time when bad powers had the upper hand. They demonstrated a true example of humane cooperation, whilst taking a huge personal risk in looking after us."

There was always the danger that the police would arrest Otto's staff and imprison them for helping the Franks. The German police offered cash rewards for the capture and arrest of hidden Jews. Tips came from collaborators, antisemitic Dutch people who sympathized with the Nazis. "It was a tense and frightening time for us, the helpers," Kugler recalled. "Our greatest fear was that the hiding place would be discovered." When the police started searching houses for hidden bicycles, Kugler thought of a way to make the annex more secure. He built a bookcase in front of the entrance. "It swings out on its hinges and opens like a door," Anne wrote. "Now our Secret Annex has truly become secret."

NINE

Amsterdam, 1942–1944

On July 13, 1942, the van Pels family moved into the secret annex. In her diary Anne renamed them "van Daan."

"From the first, we ate our meals together," she wrote, "and after three days it felt as if the seven of us had become one big family." But Peter, age sixteen, annoyed her. "He's an obnoxious boy who lies around on his bed all day, only rousing himself to do a little carpentry work before returning to his nap," she wrote. "What a dope!"

However, Otto tutored Peter along with Anne and Margot, and also taught him English. Soon Anne began to like him a little. On October 1, 1942, she wrote, "From time to time Peter can be very amusing. He and I have one thing in common: we like to dress up, which makes everyone laugh. One evening we made our appearance, with Peter in one of his mother's skin-tight dresses and me in his suit. He wore a hat; I had a cap on. The grown-ups split their sides laughing, and we enjoyed ourselves every bit as much."

In November 1942 an eighth person joined them in hiding. He was Miep's Jewish dentist, Fritz Pfeffer. At first Anne looked forward to his arrival. "Great news!" she wrote. "We're planning to take an eighth person into hiding with us! . . . We'll ask him to bring along something to fill cavities with."

Anne had to share her room with him, and Margot moved into their parents' room. Anne and Pfeffer quickly got on each other's nerves. In her diary she called him Dussel, a German word that in English translates as "idiot."

With so many people crammed together, tempers flared. Peter's mother criticized Anne for being "fresh . . . outspoken." Anne fought with her mother and felt that only her father understood her. She

Peter van Pels, age unknown

called Margot "a stinker" and described her as "a constant source of irritation, morning, noon and night."

Arguments broke out among the adults, especially over food. As the war dragged on during the "Hunger Winter" of 1944, there was a shortage of food for everyone throughout Holland. The residents of the annex learned that non-Jews *not* in hiding had nothing to eat either except tulip bulbs, potato peels, and pieces of sugar beet. Shopping became increasingly difficult for Miep, who had to stand in line for hours. "Whatever food I could find," she recalled, "was now sometimes half rotten. Regardless, I'd have to buy it anyway. We were all constantly getting stomach problems from bad food."

Anne kept herself occupied by devoting more and more time to writing. She still hoped to go to Hollywood someday and on December 24, 1943, wrote a story called "Dreams of Film Stardom." In the story the heroine, a Dutch teenager named Anne, writes a letter to Priscilla Lane, the youngest of three movie stars who were sisters. She writes in

English, just as the real-life Anne had done when she sent a pen-pal letter to Juanita. And Priscilla answers with a photo, exactly as Juanita had done, and an invitation to visit her in Hollywood for two months. The fictional parents of Anne object to her traveling alone and staying away so long. But she says, "I had made up my mind to go to America, and go I must." Priscilla arranges for her companion, Miss Halwood, to come to Amsterdam and act as Anne's chaperone. "Father and I went to the station to meet the lady," writes Anne in the story. "Father, who had once been in America and spoke good English [just as Otto Frank did], conversed with Miss Halwood, and I ventured a remark now and then. It had been arranged that she would stay with us for a week. That week fairly flew by . . .

In a scene from the 1941 movie *Four Mothers*, Rosemary Lane plays the piano, and Priscilla Lane plays the violin.

"On July 25, I was so excited that I couldn't swallow a single bite of my breakfast. But Miss Halwood, an experienced traveler, gave no sign of agitation. The entire family saw us off at Schiphol Airport, and finally, finally, my trip to America had begun."

Anne, the heroine, goes to Hollywood, stays with the Lane sisters, and lands a job as a model. After three days she finds the work exhausting and by the end of the story realizes that she no longer wants to be a film star.

The real Anne Frank had decided on another career. "My greatest wish is to be a journalist," she confided to her diary, "and later on, a famous writer . . . . After the war I'd like to publish a book called *The Secret Annex*."

During this winter Anne and Peter became better friends. Soon their friendship blossomed into a little romance. At first Anne thought that Peter was romantically interested in Margot. But on Monday, February 14, 1944, she wrote, "On Sunday morning I noticed, to my great joy (I'll be honest with you), that Peter kept looking at me. Not in the usual way . . . it made me feel wonderful inside, and that's not a feeling I should have too often." Anne and Peter confided in each other and enjoyed long conversations about their parents, "books and . . . the past."

"I sensed a strong feeling of fellowship," Anne wrote, "which I only remember having had with my girlfriends."

A few days later she wrote, "Don't think I'm in love, because I'm not, but I do have the feeling that something beautiful is going to develop between Peter and me, a kind of friendship and feeling of trust."

Anne often visited Peter in his room, despite her mother's disapproval. Together they went up to the attic and spent hours talking and gazing through the window at the chestnut tree. Anne's feelings for Peter grew stronger, and in March she wrote, "Last night I dreamed we were kissing each other." Anne still worried that Margot really liked Peter and felt left out. But Margot sent her a note saying, "I'm not jealous of you or Peter. I'm just sorry I haven't found anyone with whom to share my thoughts and feelings, and I'm not likely to in the near future." Two days later Margot wrote, "Now that you've found companionship, enjoy it as much as you can."

Anne knew that she loved Peter. "I'm sure now that Peter loves me too," she wrote, "I just don't know in what way. I can't figure out if he wants only a good friend, or if he's attracted to me as a girl or as a sister." Then, on Sunday, April 16, 1944, Anne wrote, "Remember yesterday's date, since it was a red-letter day for me. Isn't it an important day for every girl when she gets her first kiss?"

The next day, though, she questioned her behavior. "I know I'm starting at a very young age. Not even fifteen and already so independent—I'm pretty sure Margot would never kiss a boy unless there was

View through attic window in secret annex

some talk of an engagement or marriage. Neither Peter or I have any such plans."

Anne asked her father for his opinion about her relationship with Peter. Otto pointed out the difficulties they had, living close together in the annex and seeing each other every day. "Don't go upstairs so often," he told her, and "don't encourage him more than you can help. Be careful, Anne, and don't take it too seriously!"

Anne followed her father's advice and the romance with Peter cooled down. "I've distanced myself a little from the situation," she wrote.

Meanwhile, attention in the annex focused on when the American invasion would begin. "Suspense is rising to fever pitch," Anne wrote on May 22, 1944. On June 6, 1944, a broadcast came over the radio from the BBC that lifted everyone's spirits. "This is D-Day. This is *the* day. The invasion has begun!" Anne reported. The Americans had landed in Normandy, France. The BBC broadcast a speech in English by Supreme Allied Commander General Dwight D. Eisenhower, who said, "Stiff fighting will come now, but after this the victory."

"The best part about the invasion is that I have the feeling that friends are on the way," Anne wrote. "Maybe, Margot says, I can even go back to school in October or September."

On June 9 she wrote, "We're all hoping that the war will finally be over by the end of the year. It's about time!"

A week later, right before Anne's fifteenth birthday, Peter gave Miep a few coins and asked her to buy some flowers for Anne. "A few lavender peonies were all that I could find," Miep recalled. In her diary Anne mentioned this gift: "Peter gave me a lovely bouquet of peonies." Her list of birthday presents also included "Springer's five-volume art history book, a set of underwear...two honey cookies (small)... candy from Miep, candy and notebooks from Bep, and the high point: the book *Maria Theresa* and three slices of full-cream cheese from Mr. Kugler."

On July 15, 1944, after two years in hiding, she wrote, "Anyone who claims that the older folks have a more difficult time in the Annex doesn't realize that the problems have a far greater impact on *us*.

"It's difficult in times like these: ideals, dreams and cherished hopes rise within us, only to be crushed by grim reality. I hear the approaching thunder that, one day, will destroy us too, I feel the suffering of millions. And yet, when I look up at the sky, I somehow feel that everything will change for the better, that this cruelty too shall end, that peace and tranquility will return once more."

On the morning of August 4, 1944, Otto was upstairs in Peter's room helping him with an English assignment. "Suddenly someone came running up the stairs," he recalled. "Then the door opened and a man was standing right in front of us with a gun in his hand and it was pointed at us." The man was from the Gestapo, the German secret state police. He gathered everyone together and arrested all of them. He also arrested two members of Otto's staff, Kugler and Kleiman, who had helped them hide. "Get ready," he said, and gave them five minutes to collect their things.

Downstairs a member of the *Sicherheitsdienst* (SD or "secret police" who were Dutch assistants to the German police) grabbed Otto's briefcase and shook everything out on the floor—Anne's diary, the notebooks, and hundreds of loose pages with her writing. But he saw nothing of value. He then led the annex residents outside, where a police van was waiting. Anne, Margot, their parents, and the other six climbed in and were driven off to Nazi headquarters.

TEN

Iowa, 1943–1944

In July 1943 Betty saw a picture of General Dwight D. Eisenhower on the front page of *The New York Times*. Headlines announced: *Americans Battle Enemy, Allied Attacks are Imminent, Churchill Promises Blows in Europe by Fall.* Betty still worried and wondered what was happening to Anne and Margot in Amsterdam. "We never completely forgot," she said.

That summer Betty was living in Washington, D.C., with her girlfriends from Danville. They shared "two rooms and a bath . . . right up from the White House and on Embassy Row."

At first Betty and her roommates were excited about working at the FBI. Betty arrived at the Department of Justice expecting her new job to be "adventuresome." And it was, especially when she met the bureau's director, J. Edgar Hoover.

"We all were taken into J. Edgar Hoover's private office and introduced to him and shook his hand," she recalled. "I was thrilled, and didn't wash my hand until the next day. It was a big deal for kids fresh from the farm. At that time we thought well of him."

Hoover, director of the FBI since 1924, was one of the most feared and powerful men in Washington. He kept secret files on many celebrities—politicians, entertainers, writers, artists, professors—without their knowledge. Years later he was exposed for abusing his power and destroying the lives of innocent Americans. Hoover, known as the Boss, did things his own

J. Edgar Hoover working at desk during WWII

way with illegal wiretaps and hidden microphones as he investigated and attacked people whose beliefs and views differed from his own, even if they had not broken any laws.

But in 1943, when Betty went to work for him, Hoover was following direct orders from President Roosevelt to keep track of potential spies and saboteurs. Betty dreamed of becoming an FBI agent herself. However, "all I could do was type," she said. Her job consisted of typing information from thousands and thousands of big fingerprint cards onto smaller three-by-five-inch index cards. She worked in a file room the size of two football fields with hundreds of other typists.

Thousands of typists were employed by the government during the war. This photo was taken in 1942.

Hoover was known for his files—white cards for personal files, pink cards for official/confidential files. Over the years he accumulated a total of fifty-five million cards in his "general file." At the time Betty went to work for him, he kept a top-secret "restricted file" in his secretary's office so that

75

file clerks like Betty would not come across "highly sensitive material" — such as letters and photos — and gossip about what they'd seen.

On Sunday, their only day off, Betty and her friends went sightseeing. "We saw all we could, usually walking wherever we went. We saw the Lincoln Memorial, Washington Monument, Jefferson Memorial, Library of Congress, Capitol, Arlington Cemetery, and many other special sights. One day, when Churchill came to see Roosevelt and to speak to Congress, we saw them go by in a big black limosine [sic]! We were from middle America off a farm and we were excited!" Years later Betty recalled wishing she could write Margot and tell her about seeing Churchill and living in the nation's capital right near the White House.

While Betty and her friends were in D.C., the movie *Mr. Smith Goes to Washington* was playing. "We all went to see it," remembered Betty, "we were excited to be part of it." The movie tells of an ordinary person like herself, from a small town like Danville, who goes to Washington and fights for his ideals. Yet Betty quickly tired of her job just as Anne's heroine had in the story "Dreams of Film Stardom."

Woman hosing down locomotive of the Chicago and Northwestern Railway Company, Clinton, Iowa, 1943. These women employed by C & NW to clean locomotives were known as "WIPES."

"All we did every day was type 3" x 5" cards," Betty remembered, "with a goal of a minimum of 300 a day. With rooms filled to the ceiling with fingerprint cards to be done, it was an endless job. I could see no future for me if this was all I ever had time to do." So she and one of her friends who was engaged to be married quit. "We got tickets home and left at the end of the first six weeks," she wrote.

Betty returned to Iowa and enrolled in Burlington Junior College. She moved into the apartment her mother and sister were sharing. Juanita kept waitressing while she finished high school in Burlington, and their mother worked at a machine shop from three in the afternoon to eleven every night during the week. Like many women throughout the United States, Betty and Juanita's mom put on coveralls and a bandanna and switched to an industrial job. Women were now needed to do the work traditionally done by men who had "gone to war or into higher paying war plants." In Iowa the Northwestern Railway even hired women to work as "WIPES," or engine wipers. They cleaned and serviced locomotives. "At first we did not know how they'd take to the job," commented a labor foreman. "But the women soon convinced us that they look at all those dusty locomotives in the same way they do the job at a big, dirty house."

"There was a slogan," recalled Ida Belle Sands of Terril, Iowa, "Work or fight. This was a new thing for the woman and took her into new things that she had never done before—hard work, duty work, with men. It was just a complete change in lifestyle and happened practically over night. It had a lasting effect because the woman was never satisfied again to not be independent and have her paycheck." Ida Belle worked at an egg-drying plant, where she sorted eggs, cracking them open by hand and dropping them into pails. "The way that you determined whether the egg was spoiled or not was by smelling it," she said. The good ones were processed into powdered eggs and sent to servicemen overseas.

Although Betty was going to school full-time, she held various part-time jobs, working in the school office and for her chemistry professor; collecting payments for a newspaper, the *Des Moines Register*;

and doing some typing each week for the Girl Scouts. She and Juanita would also do "odd jobs for extra money and spend it on the way home. We'd go to the Maid-Rite and get a good hamburger," Betty remembered, "or get a quart of ice cream and stop at an older lady friend's house. She'd make chocolate topping, then we'd sit around the kitchen table and visit."

Betty and Juanita were both so busy working and going to school that they hardly dated. "Neither one of us was boy crazy," Betty recalled. "We ran with a lot of kids but there was no romance. We were kind of slow."

Since they were living in Burlington, a city bigger than Danville, it was easier for them to stay informed about the war. More newspapers were available, and Betty and Juanita searched the pages for any news about Amsterdam or Holland. They also had a radio. In 1943 Otto Frank's old friend Nathan Straus, Jr. had acquired radio station WMCA in New York City. That year, on Christmas Day, Straus canceled the usual programs for twenty-four hours and instead broadcast greetings from servicemen overseas to their families.

On December 25, 1943, headlines announced: *Eisenhower named Commander for Invasion; 3,000 planes smash French coast; Berlin Hit; Roosevelt promises Nation a Durable*

Front page of *The New York Times*, Tuesday, June 6, 1944

Peace. By June 1944 a map printed on the front page of *The New York Times* showed where General Eisenhower's armies had landed in Normandy. Betty and Juanita and their mother heard the same news in Iowa that the Franks heard in the secret annex: "The invasion of Europe from the west has begun." In America, as in Holland, everyone hoped that the war would soon end.

ELEVEN

Holland and Poland,

1944–1945

Around noon, on August 4, 1944, Betty sat at her desk eating a sack lunch. That summer she worked for the H. B. Green Transportation Company, a trucking firm in Burlington. Meanwhile, her sister, Juanita, was at Walgreen's drugstore waiting on customers at the counter. They had no idea what was happening that day to their pen pals in Amsterdam.

Anne, Margot, their parents, the other four who had been in hiding with them, and Kleiman and Kugler were driven to jail. It was the first time Anne and Margot had been outside in two years. When they arrived at Nazi headquarters, located in a school that had been taken over by the Gestapo, they were all locked up in a room. Otto tried to apologize to Kleiman for getting him into this dreadful situation, but his friend said, "Don't give it another thought. If it was up to me, I wouldn't have done it any differently."

Karl Josef Silberbauer, the member of the SD, or Secret Police, who had arrested them, sent Kleiman and Kugler to another cell. "At a distance," Kugler recalled, "in the corridor outside Silberbauer's office, we saw the Franks, the van Pelses and Pfeffer. All eight looked serious and troubled, not knowing what the future would bring. We waved to each other and that was good-bye."

That night Anne, Margot, and their parents were locked up in cells in the basement. The next day they were transferred to an old jail, and two days later they were sent to the train station along with hundreds of other Jewish prisoners. Two sisters in the crowd remembered noticing

A school in Amsterdam taken over as a German police headquarters

the Franks. "A very worried father and a nervous mother and two children wearing sports-type clothes and backpacks."

All prisoners boarded a regular passenger train and headed for Westerbork Transit Camp. The doors were locked and bolted behind them. Otto remembered that they were given a little food for the trip. "We knew where we were bound," he recalled, "but in spite of that it was almost as if we were once more going travelling, or having an outing, and we were actually cheerful. Cheerful, at least, when I compare this journey with our next. In our hearts, of course, we were already anticipating the possibility that we might not remain in Westerbork to the end. We knew about deportation to Poland . . . As we rode toward Westerbork we were hoping that our luck would hold."

On the train Anne stayed glued to the window, watching the scenery.

Perhaps the farms and grazing cows reminded her of Juanita's description of Danville, Iowa. "It was summer," Otto recalled. "Meadows, stubble fields and villages flew by...It was like freedom."

By late afternoon they reached Westerbork Transit Camp. A high barbed-wire fence surrounded the camp, which was like a small town. There were barracks, workshops, a school, an old people's home, a hospital, a laundry, and even a café. At night men and women were separated, but during the day they were allowed to meet and walk wherever they liked.

Karl Josef Silberbauer, the policeman who arrested the families hiding in the secret annex

Everyone registered upon arrival. Vera Cohn questioned the Franks and later remembered them well. "Mr. Frank was a pleasant-looking man, courteous and cultured. He stood before me tall and erect. He answered my routine questions quietly. Anne was by his side. Her face, by certain standards, was not a pretty one, but her eyes—bright, young, eager eyes—made you look at her again. She was fifteen then. None of the Franks showed any signs of despair over their plight. Their composure, as they grouped around my typing desk in the receiving room, was one of quiet dignity."

Peter, his parents, and Fritz Pfeffer had been sent to Westerbork on the same train. Since they had all been in hiding, they were labeled "convict Jews" and placed in the "punishment block." They had fewer privileges than other prisoners. Their clothes were taken away from them and they had to wear blue overalls with red shoulder patches, and wooden clogs. Men had their heads shaved and women had their hair cut short. And they were given less food than everyone else and assigned to harder jobs.

Westerbork Transit Camp, the Netherlands

Adults did industrial work, just as women were doing in America. But whereas people like Betty and Juanita's mother were contributing to the American war effort, prisoners at Westerbork were forced to help the Germans. They took apart old airplane batteries and cleaned them. It was dirty work. "We looked like coal miners," recalled a prisoner. Otto tried to get Anne a slightly better job of cleaning toilets but failed. So Anne, along with her sister and mother, scraped paste from the batteries. The toxic fumes made them cough. But the women enjoyed sitting together and talking while they worked. Although Anne had quarreled with her mother and sister while they lived in the secret annex, she clung to them at Westerbork. "They were very close together, they always walked together," remembered Ronnie Goldstein-van Cleef, a woman prisoner.

Anne resumed her tender relationship with Peter. "I saw Anne Frank and Peter van Pels every day in Westerbork," recalled another prisoner, Rosa de Winter. "They were always together . . . Anne was so

Westerbork Transit Camp was extremely overcrowded.

lovely, so radiant...her movements, her looks, had such a lilt to them that I often asked myself, Can she possibly be happy? She was happy in Westerbork, though that seems almost incredible."

Eva, the girl who had lived in Anne's neighborhood and had so much wanted to be friends with her, Sanne, and Hanneli, was also imprisoned at Westerbork that summer. She remembered feeling hopeful. "It wasn't a concentration camp and we thought we might stay there until the liberation."

"It was a particular relief for the children to no longer be locked away and to be able to talk with other people," Otto said. "We, the old ones, however, feared the danger of being transported to the rumoured death camps of Poland."

Every Tuesday a transport of about a thousand prisoners left for the east. On the night of September 2, 1944, a section leader and a German official entered the punishment barracks and announced the names of those who would be deported the next day. Among those called were Peter and his parents; Fritz Pfeffer; and Otto, Edith, Margot, and Anne Frank.

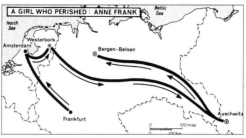

Anne's route through Europe starting with her birth place, Frankfurt, Germany and ending in Bergen-Belsen

The next morning they boarded the train, a cattle car lined with straw. The Franks, the van Pels family, and Pfeffer stayed in the same boxcar, squeezed together with about sixty other people. They had no food, only a bucket of water and another bucket to be used as a toilet. No one knew exactly where they were going, but rumors spread that they were headed for Auschwitz–Birkenau Concentration Camp in Poland. At night they could not sleep because of fear and the bad smell. "Many people, among them the Frank girls, leaned against their father or mother," recalled a passenger; "everyone was dead tired."

Roll call at Auschwitz-Birkenau, Poland

In his memoir Otto wrote: "The awful transportation—three days locked in a cattle truck—was the last time I saw my family. Each of us tried to be as courageous as possible and not to let our heads drop."

They arrived at Auschwitz at night. "The first we saw of Auschwitz were the glaring searchlights fixed on the train," recalled Rosa. "We stumbled out and I had the feeling I had arrived in hell. Chimneys were burning with huge bright flames. The SS beat everybody with sticks and guns." A voice over the loudspeaker screamed, "Women to the left! Men to the right!"

Some of the six hundred children and young people under the age of eighteen found alive in Auschwitz when the camp was liberated by the Russians. The children show their prisoner numbers tattooed on their arms.

Next came the selection. The Nazis decided who was fit to work and who would immediately be gassed. Anne, Margot, their mother, and Rosa were forced to march quickly to the women's camp and were assigned to the same barracks. Each prisoner had a number tattooed on her arm. Then they were sprayed with delousing powder, had their heads shaved, and showered with cold water. The women wore only thin gray sacks. One day Anne somehow got hold of a pair of men's long underwear. "She looked screamingly funny with those long white legs," recalled Rosa, "but somehow still charming."

The Nazis took roll call at different times of night or day, in all kinds of weather. Ronnie, who had known Anne and Margot at Westerbork, said they often stood next to each other and shared a mug of so-called coffee. "We used the same little cup and passed it to each other," she said. "Margot was close by, next to [Anne] or in front of her, depending on how it worked out because you stood in rows of five. Anne was very calm and quiet and somewhat withdrawn. The fact that they had ended up there had affected her profoundly—that was obvious."

Their work consisted of hauling stones and digging up grassy clumps of earth. At night they received a slice of bread and a tiny piece of margarine. "Anne was the youngest in her group," remembered Rosa, "but nevertheless she was the leader of it. She also distributed the bread in the barracks, and she did it so well and so fairly that there was none of the usual grumbling." Anne, Margot, and their mother stayed close, taking care of one another. "Mrs. Frank was always near her chil-

dren and saw to it that they had something to eat," remembered Ronnie. "Mrs. Frank tried very hard to keep her children alive, to keep them with her, to protect them."

But on October 30, 1944, another selection took place. Anne and Margot were forced to go on a transport and their mother was left behind in Auschwitz. "The children! O, God, the children...!" screamed Edith as her daughters were taken away.

Map of the Nazi Concentration Camps

TWELVE

Germany, 1944–1945

Auschwitz was behind them now, and their mother as well. After a four-day train ride with hardly any food or water, Anne and Margot reached the concentration camp of Bergen-Belsen in Germany. New prisoners stayed in tents. Anne and Margot went to wash from a tap of water up on a hill and met two other Dutch girls, also sisters—Lientje and Janny. When the girls asked Anne and Margot about their mother, "Anne began to cry bitterly." The four friends sat huddled together, watching other newcomers arrive. "The two [Anne and Margot] were inseparable, like my sister and I," recalled Lientje. "They looked like two frozen birds, it was painful to look at them. After we had washed, naked in the open air, we were speedily dressed, for we had nothing except a dress and a thin blanket, a blanket which one treasured like a costly possession."

By December 1944 Anne and Margot had wound up in the same barracks as Lientje and Janny, and slept on a wooden bunk below theirs. "Anne used to tell stories after we lay down," remembered Lientje. "So did Margot. Silly stories and jokes. We all took turns

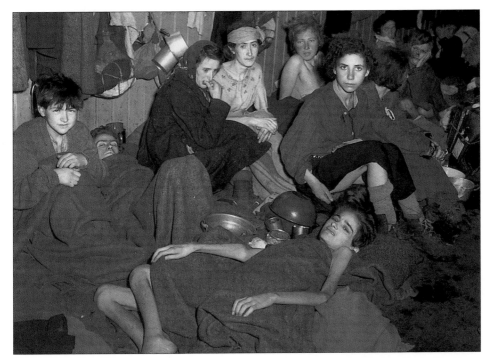

Women and children, many of whom were suffering from typhus, huddle together in a barracks at Bergen-Belsen after their liberation in April 1945.

telling them. Mostly they were about food. Once we talked about going to the American Hotel in Amsterdam for dinner and Anne suddenly burst into tears at the thought that we would never get back...we compiled a menu, masses of wonderful things to eat.

"Anne and I began to 'organize' things, to steal from the kitchen or to beg. If you were caught, this meant a beating, but we were not caught. We never stole from another prisoner; we stole from the Nazis."

At the end of December, Anne, Margot, and their friends knew it was Christmas and Hanukkah. "We saved scraps from our scanty bread ration and received a special ration of one quarter of a Harz cheese," recalled Lientje. "Anne had found a small piece of garlic somewhere. I had sung some songs in another block and been rewarded with a little sauerkraut. The Daniels sisters, with whom we were together, had organized a beetroot and a carrot. With our six blankets we improvised a table and with these ingredients we made a Christmas feast, Anne said, 'And we are celebrating *Hanukkah* at the same time.'"

Together they sang Jewish songs. Then Anne told stories. "We thought they must be old stories which we did not happen to know," remembered Lientje. "But now I know they were stories that Anne had made up herself. Margot started to tell a story too, but she could not go on and Anne completed it for her. She said that her father knew much better stories and Margot began to cry, asking whether he was still alive. Anne was confident, 'Of course he is alive.'"

But soon she began to think that both her parents were dead. Anne and Margot were moved to another part of the camp and Anne discovered that her good friend Hanneli was there. They arranged to speak one night for a few minutes from either side of the barbed-wire fence.

Hanneli told Anne that she thought Anne had gone to Switzerland. Anne told Hanneli how they had really been in hiding, then imprisoned at Auschwitz. "She told me that her father had been killed," remembered Hanneli, "her mother too, she thought."

Since Hanneli was an "exchange prisoner" (she, her father, and little sister had Paraguayan passports and might be exchanged by the Nazis for German prisoners of war), she was allowed to receive Red Cross packages. The next night, she tossed a bundle of food to Anne over the fence, but another woman caught it and would not give it up. Hanneli tried again the following night, and this time Anne got the package that contained Swedish bread, dried fruit, and a pair of socks. The girls planned to meet again but never did.

In March of 1945 Anne and Margot came down with typhus, a disease raging through the concentration camp. Thousands died every day. Anne and Margot lay huddled together in a cold, drafty bunk near the barracks door. They screamed, "Close the door! Close the door! Close the door!" recalled Rachel van Amerongen-Frankfoorder, another prisoner who had also known them at Westerbork. "They were so cold, just like the rest of us . . . Day by day they got weaker."

Lientje came to visit them. "Margot had fallen from the bunk and was half-unconscious," she remembered. "Anne was already very feverish. She was very friendly and loving. 'Margot will sleep well and when she sleeps I don't need to get up anymore. . . . ' Anne said. 'Oh, I'm so nice and warm,' and she seemed quite happy."

Margot died sometime that month. Without her sister or parents, Anne felt that she had nothing to live for and gave up hope. She did not know that although her mother had died at Auschwitz in January, her father had been liberated in February and was frantically searching for news of his wife and children. In mid or late March, Anne Frank died alone. A short time later, on April 15, 1945, British troops liberated Bergen-Belsen.

THIRTEEN

iowa and illinois, 1945

In Burlington Betty and Juanita read the newspapers but knew little if anything about the death camps in Europe. Articles such as "Tragedy of a People" and "Nazis Seek to Rid Europe of All Jews" appeared occasionally but were tucked away in the middle sections of the papers and were hardly noticed. Most Americans who did read these articles did not believe accounts of Nazi atrocities. It did not seem possible that the Nazis intended to systematically kill *all* Jews.

"Little did we know the truth," said Betty years later.

On April 11, 1945, General Patton's troops had marched into Buchenwald, the first concentration camp liberated by the Americans. "They discovered a hell they had known absolutely nothing about," wrote Elie Wiesel, a survivor. "When the children with dead eyes and skeletal faces looked at them, all they could do was lower their heads and weep." Photojournalist Margaret Bourke-White accompanied General Patton and took pictures that were published in *Life*. In those days, before television was widely available, photomagazines such as *Life* and *Look* printed pictures to illustrate articles about current events,

Evacuating female political prisoners from Bergen-Belsen, April 28, 1945

allowing readers to see for themselves the stories covered.

On April 15 the British liberated Bergen-Belsen, the concentration camp in which Anne and Margot had died. Photographs show survivors peeling potatoes near piles of corpses and a British soldier clearing corpses with a bulldozer. Young soldiers were shocked and horrified by what they saw. "Many will bear the mental scars of the experience to their dying day," stated an article in *The Reader's Digest*.

Americans, even Jews, still could not grasp the enormity of the crime.

As the war in Europe seemed to be drawing to a close, Betty and Juanita read the news and thought about Anne and Margot.

President Franklin D. Roosevelt died of a cerebral hemorrhage at Warm Springs, Georgia, on April 12, 1945, and "it hit the Americans hard," reported *The Reader's Digest*. "His death devastated civilians and the armed forces alike." Vice President Harry Truman was sworn in at the White House and became the new president. By the end of April, Hitler realized that the Germans had lost the war. On April 30 he killed himself, and on May 2 German troops surrendered to the western Allies.

The War in Europe Is Ended! proclaimed *The New York Times* on May 8, 1945. Americans everywhere celebrated VE (Victory in Europe) day.

That spring Betty graduated from junior college. Her former teacher Miss Birdie sent her a note of congratulations and wrote, "May success attend you in all your efforts." Betty, Juanita, and their mother moved to Denver, Colorado. Betty and her mother got jobs on the assembly line at a tire company. "But our room, and the hard sofa I slept on had bed bugs," Betty recalled. So five weeks later they returned to Iowa. Juanita got her old job waitressing at Walgreen's, moved into the YWCA, and stayed in Burlington to finish high school. Betty and her mother went to Rock Island, Illinois, and looked for jobs.

That summer, on August 7, the United States dropped the first atomic bomb on Hiroshima, Japan. A second bomb hit Nagasaki two days later. On Wednesday, August 15, headlines read *Japan surrenders, End of War!*

"When the war ended in 1945, I was in Rock Island, working at a cardboard box factory," recalled Betty. Now that the war was finally over, she wrote to Anne and Margot at their old Amsterdam address, the only one she had. "I was not at all sure they would get my letter or

Juanita, age sixteen, 1946

respond," she said. "All during the war we wondered where they were and how they were getting along. Were they alive? Did they have enough food?"

In early September, Otto received Betty's letter and wrote about it to his mother who still lived in Switzerland. "Some days ago, a long letter from America arrived for Margot and Anne from a girl with whom they had had no actual contact," he wrote. "This girl wanted to start their correspondence again. I wrote to her in floods of tears. Things like that upset me very much. But it doesn't matter."

By this time Otto knew that his wife had died in Auschwitz and his daughters had died at Bergen-Belsen.

During this period, Betty and her mother stopped working at the cardboard factory. Her mother again became a teacher at a country school and asked the county superintendent to give Betty an "emergency certificate" since there was a shortage of teachers. Betty was offered a position at Tindall #1, a school in a small Illinois town called

Milan. She accepted and moved in with a family who lived across the field from the school.

"It turned out that I had twenty-eight students in eight grades," she recalled. "The first week was very trying and when Mom came by on Friday night from her school to get me, I was in tears, and I wanted to quit."

But Betty's mother urged her to stick with it. "She told me that I couldn't quit. I had started this job and I had to finish it."

After a weekend visit in Danville, seeing her sister and fixing up their farmhouse, Betty returned to Tindall #1

Tindall #1, one-room schoolhouse, Milan, Illinois

in better spirits. That fall she heard from Otto Frank. "When I received the letter I shed tears," Betty recalled.

"It was a long four or five page handwritten letter detailing their experiences during the war. About how they lived in the attic 25 months before the Germans came and took them to the prison camps, and how only Otto survived. His wife and Anne and Margot died from malnutrition and disease just before the war ended.

"This was the first inkling we had that they were Jewish, or we'd have been more concerned than ever during those 'quiet' years. I shared the letter with my children at school. I wanted them to know what they had missed by living in America during the worst war anyone had ever known."

FOURTEEN

Amsterdam, 1945

After liberation from Auschwitz, Otto slowly made his way back to Amsterdam. He had miraculously survived by staying behind in the camp hospital, too sick and weak to be evacuated with other prisoners in the middle of January 1945. The Russians had liberated Auschwitz on January 27, and nurses had taken care of Otto and hundreds of others.

By February he was strong enough to write to his mother and sister in Switzerland and his brother, Robert, in England. "Where Edith and the children are, I do not know. We have been apart since 5 September 1944. One has to be hopeful." Otto returned to Amsterdam by way of Russia. At a stop in Poland, he found out from one of his wife's friends at Auschwitz that Edith had died in January. "Mr. Frank did not move when I told him," the friend recalled. "I looked into his face, but he had turned away."

On May 2, 1945, Otto sailed from Odessa, Russia, to Marseille, France. From there he took a train and arrived in Amsterdam on June 3. He went directly to Miep and Jan Gies's apartment. Miep rushed out to greet him. "We looked at each other," she recalled. "There were no words. He was thin, but he'd always been thin. 'Miep,' he said quietly. 'Miep, Edith is not coming back . . . but I have great hope for Anne and Margot.'"

Otto stayed with Miep and Jan. The next day he went to 263 Prinsengracht and visited with other old friends— Kugler and Kleiman, who had both sur-vived. Kugler had

Otto Frank (standing on the right) reunited with his brothers and sister in Switzerland after the war.

escaped from a death march from a concentration camp, and Kleiman had been released from a transit camp because of severe stomach problems. Miep had run the business for Otto in his absence and now he went back to work. "I go to the office daily because that's the only way to divert myself," he wrote to his sister and brother-in-law on June 21. "I just can't think how I could go on without the children, having lost Edith already... It's too upsetting for me to write about them. Naturally I still hope, and wait, wait, wait."

Otto kept searching for news of Anne and Margot.

On June 29 Otto's brother-in-law Julius sent him a letter from Leominster, Massachusetts. "My last hope is that you will find the children," he wrote. "Walter and I will do everything for you. In case you want to come to the USA we have money saved for you three. Send

97

me a cable when you have found the children...Let me know if you need food. We will send it."

Julius sent him another letter a few days later. "The destiny of the two girls is on my mind day and night," he wrote. "Please inform us at once...when you hear of them. Wishing you all luck."

On July 18, 1945, Otto finally found out what had happened to Anne and Margot. He saw their names on a Red Cross list with symbols of crosses indicating that they were dead. He discovered that the woman who had made the marks was named Lientje, and that she and her sister, Janny, had known his daughters at Bergen-Belsen. Otto immediately traveled to the town where the sisters lived to talk with them. In his memoir he wrote, "My friends, who had been hopeful with me, now mourned with me. It took many months for me to get used to a normal life without my loved ones."

At last Miep told Otto that after he and the others were arrested, she had gone back to the secret annex and had gathered up all of Anne's

writings—her diary with the plaid cover, notebooks, and loose sheets of office paper. Miep had taken Anne's writings downstairs to the office and had locked them up without reading a word. "I reached into the drawer on the side of my desk and took out the papers that had been waiting there for

Anne's original diary, given to her on her thirteenth birthday, June 12, 1942

Anne for nearly a year now," Miep recalled. "No one, including me, had touched them. Now Anne was not coming back for the diary.

"I took out all the papers, placing the little red-orange checkered diary on top, and carried everything into Mr. Frank's office.

"Frank was sitting at his desk, his eyes murky with shock. I held out the diary and the papers to him. I said, 'Here is your daughter Anne's legacy to you.'"

FIFTEEN

amsterdam 1945–1956

At first Otto could not bear to read Anne's diary. But in September of 1945, after spending *Rosh Hashanah*, the Jewish New Year, with Anne's old friend Hanneli who had survived and returned to Holland, he felt ready. "I began to read slowly," Otto wrote, "only a few pages each day, more would have been impossible, as I was overwhelmed by painful memories. For me it was a revelation. I had no idea of the depth of her thoughts and feelings. I had never imagined how intensely Anne had occupied her mind with the problem and meaning of Jewish suffering over the centuries, and the power she had gained through her belief in God. I also read how important her relationship with Peter had been."

In a letter to his sister, Leni, Otto wrote: "What I'm reading in her [Anne's] book is so indescribably exciting. Even if it hadn't been written by her, it would have interested me."

And on September 30, 1945, he wrote to his mother, "I can't put Anne's diary down. The diary I *never* allow out of my sight because there is so much in it that no one else should read. But I will make excerpts from this."

Otto started typing the diary in German, selecting certain parts he thought were appropriate, omitting others. He left out Anne's sexual observations, for example, and her criticisms of her mother. Otto's friend Anneliese Schutz helped him with the translation. Anne had written her diary and stories in Dutch, but Otto's mother knew only German. "He worked on this every evening," recalled Miep. "He sent these sections to his mother in Basel [Switzerland]."

Otto kept asking Miep to listen to bits of the diary, but she could not. "It was much too upsetting to me," she recalled.

But Otto started telling others about it. He showed the diary to Jacque, Anne's best friend, now sixteen years old. Jacque's family had survived and still lived in the River Quarter. "Otto Frank came by practically every day," Jacque recalled. "He talked about Anne and the diary she had written while hiding on the Prinsengracht. Then he also gave me the two letters from Anne. The first was her farewell letter to me. The second was her reply to a letter that I'd actually never written. I was so touched by her words and overcome with such emotion."

Otto also showed the diary to Eva, the girl who had wanted to be friends with Anne, and her mother, Fritzi Geiringer. They had all been imprisoned in Auschwitz and had briefly met. "He read a few pages from it, and he burst into tears," recalled Eva.

In November 1945 Otto wrote in a letter to his old friend Nathan Straus, Jr. in New York, "Apart from business I am very busy in copying the diary of my

Jacqueline (Jacque) van Maarsen with Otto Frank, photograph taken in Basel in 1970 youngest daughter (which was found by chance), and to find an editor for it. I am going to let you know more about it later."

One Sunday, when Otto invited friends over for coffee at the apartment he shared with Miep and Jan, he mentioned the diary. One of his guests, a German Jewish refugee with connections in publishing, asked to read it. Otto's friend then showed the diary to a historian he knew, who was equally impressed. The historian wrote an article about it and called his piece "A Child's Voice." It was published on April 3, 1946, in *Het Parool*, a Dutch newspaper that had been an important underground paper during World War II. Immediately afterward publishers began to contact Otto. He had been trying to find a publisher, but now he wondered whether he should make the diary public.

He discussed the matter with Jacque. "Why would anyone be interested in the confessions of such a young child?" she said. "And who wanted to hear anything more about the war at that point?"

Nevertheless, Otto finally decided to go ahead. "Anne would have so much loved to see something published," he wrote. "My friends' opinion was that I had no right to view this as a private legacy as it is a meaningful document about humanity."

Otto asked Jacque to write an introduction about her friendship with Anne, but she refused. "I told him that I could not imagine anyone being interested in the fact that Anne had read *Joop ter Heul* with her best friend, played Monopoly, or collected pictures of movie stars," recalled Jacque in her book *My Friend Anne Frank*. "Many years went by before I could read *Het Achterhuis* [*The Annex*] objectively and understand why it struck such a responsive chord in people around the world."

On June 25, 1947, Anne's diary was published in Dutch with the title *Het Achterhuis* (*The Annex*). The first edition had a printing of fifteen hundred copies. "When I received the first edition of Anne's diary from her father in 1947," wrote Jacque, "I had the feeling that I was reading something that was not meant for me to read." Yet she later said, "The first publication of the diary... is very close to my heart. The diary texts in this version appear, for the most part, the way Anne herself had rewritten them with the idea in mind of being published."

The book sold out in six months and went into a second printing. Otto received fan mail from children and adults. "Mr. Frank answered each letter," recalled Miep, who had still not read the diary. "Miep, you must read Anne's writings," he kept saying. "'All right,'" Miep said, "'only when I'm totally alone.'" The next day she took the book to her room and shut the door. "With awful fear in my heart, I opened the book and turned to the first page," Miep recalled. "I read the whole diary without stopping. From the first word, I heard Anne's voice come back to speak to me from where she had gone. She was alive again in my mind. When I had read the last word, I didn't feel the pain I'd anticipated. My young friend had left a remarkable legacy to the world."

The diary was translated into French, then English. In 1952, with the help of Nathan Straus, Jr., it was published in Great Britain and America under the title *Anne Frank: The Diary of a Young Girl* with a picture of Anne on the cover. Eleanor Roosevelt, widow of President Franklin D. Roosevelt and a friend of Straus's, wrote a foreword for both English-language editions. Meyer Levin, a journalist, novelist, and critic, gave the book a rave review in *The New York Times*, describing it as the voice of "six million vanished Jewish souls." Levin had originally read the French edition of the diary and was so moved that he had also helped Otto bring the book to its American publisher, Doubleday.

The book was also published in Japan in 1952 and sold more than one hundred thousand copies. The Japanese considered Anne "an acceptable and accessible culture figure of the war—a young victim, but one who inspired hope for the future."

During this time, Otto developed a closer friendship with Fritzi, Eva's mother. Fritzi had also lost loved ones; both her husband and son had been murdered at Auschwitz. "Otto and I found that we had a lot in common," she recalled. They often went to Friday night services at synagogue together. Otto took an interest in Eva and helped her find work in London at a photo studio. When she married in 1952, he was a witness at her wedding.

In April 1953 Otto resigned from his business, Opekta, and moved in with his sister and brother-in-law in Basel, Switzerland. "I live in

Exterior of the Anne Frank House as it looks today

Basel today because I can no longer live in Amsterdam," he said. "I often go there, but I can't stand it for more than three days. Then I go to the Prinsengracht where we hid for two years. Sometimes I look at our hiding place; it has not been changed. I look around and then I leave. I cannot bear the sight any longer."

In 1953 the building was almost sold, but Otto persuaded Opekta to buy it. Then in 1954 another broker bought the property and proposed to tear it down. The Dutch newspapers protested: "The Secret Annex...has become a monument to a time of oppression and man-hunts, terror and darkness. Netherlands will be subject to a national scandal if this house is pulled down..." Then in 1955 the Berghaus company purchased 263 Prinsengracht and gave it as a gift to the Anne Frank Stichting (Foundation). Through donations the corner houses next door were bought and added. On May 3, 1960, the Anne Frank House, a museum and study center, was opened. A restoration project began for the front house, but Otto insisted that the annex remain empty, just as it was after the arrest.

In November 1953 Otto married Fritzi. She settled in Switzerland with him and devoted herself to helping him with the vast correspondence related to Anne's diary.

The publication of the diary in English had been an enormous success. Producers bid on rights for dramatizing the book for the stage and Cheryl Crawford won. She offered Meyer Levin a chance to write the first script. At first Crawford liked his adaptation, but upon a second reading decided that it did not have "enough theatrical potential." So she asked producer Kermit Bloomgarden to look at it and give his opinion. He agreed with her assessment that the script was not "dramatic enough." Otto, too, agreed that Levin was not the right person for the project. "My confidence in Levin's script was vanishing," he wrote to Fritzi while on a trip to New York. In his version, Levin had exaggerated the Franks' Jewishness. "It was not so much a play as a series of religious celebrations," recalled the Doubleday editor of the diary.

Levin angrily threatened to sue Crawford, and she withdrew from the project. Bloomgarden took over and asked screenwriters Frances Goodrich and Albert Hackett, known for their

From left, foreground: Frances Goodrich, Albert Hackett, Otto Frank, and Garson Kanin. Behind them are Johannes Kleiman and Fritzi Frank, Otto's second wife.

Otto Frank, on the left, and Joseph Schildkraut portraying Otto, on the right

light comedies, to adapt the diary for the stage. Goodrich and Hackett traveled to Amsterdam to meet with Otto and to see the annex at 263 Prinsengracht. There they spent "a long and highly emotional day with Otto Frank." Although they based their script on the diary, they toned down Anne's Jewishness and made her character more universal. Goodrich and Hackett wanted the play to be uplifting and entertaining, and to appeal to audiences everywhere.

Levin was furious. He believed that his version of the diary was truer to Anne's writings. He took out an ad in the *New York Post* attacking the Goodrich and Hackett script and asked that his version be judged by the public.

The battle raged on. Levin started a lawsuit against Otto and Crawford, the first producer. Then he began a second lawsuit against Otto and Bloomgarden. Otto became disgusted with him. "I told you that it is against the ideas and ideals of Anne to have disputes and quarrels, disagreements and suing," he wrote to Levin. "I would be very much pleased if you would stop with every kind of trouble-making as this is unjust and below your standing."

In the meantime, after many rewrites, the Goodrich and Hackett script was approved and *The Diary of Anne Frank* went into rehearsal. Director Garson Kanin chose actor Joseph Schildkraut to play the part of Otto. Schildkraut had a striking resemblance to him. "I look exactly like a twin brother of Otto Frank," he commented. Born and raised in Vienna, Schildkraut spoke with a slight accent that was just right for the part. But even more important, he seemed to embody Otto's spirit. From New York, he exchanged letters with Otto, asking detailed questions. Otto sent the actor a photo of himself with one of his shirtsleeves rolled up, revealing his Auschwitz tattoo. Schildkraut kept the photo on his dressing table at the theater and studied it for inspiration. "Each night before I make my entrance," he said, "I think I'm Otto Frank." They finally met in Chicago after the play was running for a year.

The search for an actress to play the part of Anne proved more difficult. Kanin and Bloomgarden wanted a very young girl. She, like all the cast members, had to be Jewish. More than a hundred

Otto had this picture taken especially for Joseph Schildkraut.

girls were considered before Kanin and Bloomgarden chose sixteen-year-old Susan Strasberg.

The play opened on Broadway on October 5, 1955. In a letter to the cast and crew, Otto explained why he could not attend: "For me," he wrote, "this play is part of my life and the idea that my wife and children and I will be presented on the stage is a painful one to me. Therefore it is impossible for me to come and see it."

The play was a smash hit. Audiences loved it. They found it moving, charming, even humorous. Critics gave *The Diary of Anne Frank* glowing reviews. Otto's friend Nathan Straus, Jr. came to opening night, and after the performance he sent Schildkraut a cable: "Congratulations on a magnificent portrayal! You have the voice, the manner and the very personality of Otto—who is and was one of my most cherished friends. I am deeply moved—I would like to tell you so face to face." Straus did meet Schildkraut, and they became good

Susan Strasberg and Joseph Schildkraut as Anne and Otto, dancing onstage in *The Diary of Anne Frank*

friends. In 1956 the play *The Diary of Anne Frank* won the Pulitzer Prize, the Tony Award for Best Play of the Season, and the Drama Critics' Circle Award.

Otto wrote to Schildkraut "I must admit that I am surprised that the large American public, whom we Europeans imagine as preferring the 'sensational' or 'decorative theatre,' are so deeply touched by the simplicity, the purity and truth, that marks this work. May I thank you with my whole heart, for your dedicated beautiful performance, with which you help Anne's spirit to reach out into the great world."

SIXTEEN

california and iowa,

1956–1957

On May 14, 1956, Betty was driving home from work at Aerojet in Azusa, California. She, Juanita, and their mother had moved to southern California. "This had been a dream of hers [Mom's] for many years," recalled Betty. "We all decided to close up things and head west." First they lived with friends, then they bought their own little house in Sierra Madre, near Pasadena. Juanita got married and had two sons. But Betty remained in the house with their mother.

On the night of May 14, Betty was heading home and turned on her car radio. "I was listening to the news as usual," she recalled. "All at once I realized they were saying, '*The Diary of Anne Frank* is a Broadway hit in New York. It is the story of a young girl who hid in an attic with her parents in Holland during the war.' In an instant I knew it was the same Anne Frank.

"When I got into the house . . . I told Mom to put the supper on the back burner. I rushed upstairs in the carport and located Anne's letter and the pictures, etc. Her father's letter was gone! But I still knew it was the same." Juanita had given Betty permission to take charge of the correspondence, and she had placed everything in an old shoe box.

"Mom and I hurried to Vroman's bookstore before it closed that night to buy the book *The Diary of Anne Frank*," Betty remembered. "When we got it, the front cover of the book had the almost identical picture that she had sent to Juanita. What a thrill... to see a picture of Anne on the cover so similar to the one she had mailed to us. What an emotional and humbling experience to read her diary.

Ann Wagner, Betty and Juanita's mother, on the porch in Sierra Madre, California, 1947

"Mom and I read the book that night and shed some tears. Then we shared the book with other friends and told them we had letters from Anne and Margot. No one was impressed!"

Betty immediately sent a letter to their former teacher Miss Birdie, telling her about Juanita's pen pal and the diary. Miss Birdie had retired

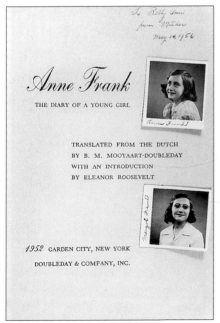

The title page from Betty's copy of *Anne Frank: The Diary of a Young Girl*, showing the photographs she and her sister had received years before

but still lived in Danville and kept her own detailed diaries about her everyday life. On May 21, 1956, she wrote, "A half inch of rain fell last night. Sent for 3 more pairs of plastic curtains. Had a letter from Betty Wagner telling of former pen pals she and Juanita had in 1940 as a result of my program of international correspondence. These girls and their parents hid in an attic from the Germans following the invasion of Holland. The family was then discovered and put in concentration camps where all except the father died by the time the war was over. One girl kept a diary which her father had published. Betty advised me to read it."

SEVENTEEN

Amsterdam, 1956–1986

The play *The Diary of Anne Frank* opened in Germany in October 1956 and had an enormous impact. A reviewer wrote, "In Berlin, after the final curtain, the audience sat in stunned silence. There was no applause. Only the welling sound of deep sobs broke the absolute still-ness. Then, still not speaking and seeming not to look at each other, the Berliners filed out of the theatre."

The German actor who played the part of Otto received many fan letters. One man who had just seen the play wrote, "I never knew what it meant [being a Nazi] until the other night." Sometimes German teenagers stayed after the performance for discussions. They asked, "How could it have happened?"

The Dutch-language version of the play premiered in Amsterdam on November 27, 1956. Otto attended the opening ceremony with Miep, Jan, Jacque, and Margot's friend Jetteke. "It was a strange sen-sation for me," recalled Jacque. "I thought that it was an impressive performance, but it was not Anne standing there on the stage, no mat-ter how well it was played. Queen Juliana also attended the premiere.

Millie Perkins and Joseph Schildkraut as Anne and Otto in the film adaptation, *The Diary of Anne Frank*

Mr. Frank never wanted to see the play."

Otto gave Goodrich and Hackett permission to write a screenplay based on the diary. In May 1957 he signed a contract for the movie with Twentieth Century Fox. George Stevens, the director, met with Otto in Amsterdam and visited the annex. Stevens had the annex faithfully re-created to scale on the set since most of the shooting took place in Hollywood. Otto and Kleiman were technical advisers and provided information and articles to make the film authentic.

In the movie Joseph Schildkraut repeated his performance as Otto. The role of Anne went to a newcomer, nineteen-year-old model Millie Perkins. "Millie is most like Anne in temperament," said Stevens. He wanted his movie to have mass appeal. "It will tell the valiant, often humorous story of a wonderful family hiding out in a time of great stress," he said, "the story of a teenage girl's magnificent triumph over fear. Her diary isn't the book of a young girl looking death in the face. It's the story of someone facing life."

Thus, Anne's dream of "a chance to come to Hollywood" was fulfilled.

The film was a box-office hit in the United States. It received eight Oscar nominations and was awarded three. However, some reviewers criticized Stevens for sentimentalizing Anne's diary. In Amsterdam the film premiered on April 16, 1959. "All of us were again invited," recalled Miep. "Queen Juliana and her daughter Crown Princess

Simon Wiesenthal in his office, 1967

Beatrix were present. As far as I know, Otto Frank never saw the play or the movie. He did not want to."

Release of the film and productions of the play worldwide increased sales of the book. Income from the diary provided Otto and his wife with a comfortable living, but he split most of the royalties between the Anne Frank House in Amsterdam and the ANNE FRANK-Fonds, established in 1963 in Basel. "The purpose of the foundation," explained Jacque, "was to combat discrimination, using the persecution of the Jews as an example—for which Anne served as a symbol—and to further Anne's ideals as they were left to the world in her diary. The money was also to be given to charitable causes with more or less the same purpose." The foundation, particularly geared for educating young people, presented rotating exhibits and provided information related to events of World War II.

When the Anne Frank House opened to visitors in 1960, students conducted tours of the annex. Otto said that he intended the house as "neither a museum nor a place of pilgrimage. It is an earnest warning from the past and a mission of hope for the future."

In 1963 Nazi hunter Simon Wiesenthal, a Holocaust survivor himself, tracked down the member of the Gestapo who had arrested the Franks and the others who were hiding. His name was Karl Josef Silberbauer. Wiesenthal had begun his hunt in 1958 when he encountered a group of teenagers handing out neo-Nazi (a contemporary fringe group inspired by Adolf Hitler's Nazis) leaflets. They challenged the authenticity of Anne's diary and said they would believe it was true if Wiesenthal could find the man who had arrested her.

When the news broke, Silberbauer was suspended from the police department in Vienna, where he worked and lived, and an investigation was launched. Upon questioning, Silberbauer said that he had received a tip from an anonymous betrayer just before he arrested the Franks and the others in hiding. Who was the betrayer? people wondered. Speculations arose. The main suspect seemed to be Willem Gerard van Maaren, a man who had worked in the Opekta warehouse and had stolen merchandise. But van Maaren kept asserting his innocence. After a year the investigation was closed for lack of further evidence.

Miep reading Anne's book

Otto did not help in the search. He said he had no wish for recrimination. Instead, he dedicated the rest of his life to promoting Anne's writings and ideals. Once he told Nathan Straus's son Peter, "In the normal family relationship, it is the child of the famous parent who has the honour and the burden of continuing the task. In my case the role is reversed."

On August 19, 1980, Otto died of cancer. He bequeathed Anne's diary to the Netherlands State Institute for War Documentation (NIOD). In 1986 the NIOD published *The Critical Edition* in Dutch to give readers a chance to compare the original entries in the handwritten diary with subsequent versions. Five new pages were discovered in 1998. They were in the possession of Otto's acquaintance Cornelius Suijk, who claimed that Otto gave him the material for safekeeping because it contained Anne's unfair criticisms of her mother and of her parents' marriage. Suijk sold the pages to the NIOD, and they were published in 2001 in an updated edition. Anne wrote the pages on

A few of the translations of Anne Frank's *The Diary of a Young Girl*

loose sheets of paper and they included an introduction to the diary. The diary has been published in seventy languages and is one of the world's best-selling books. Despite the impact it has had on millions of readers, Miep said, "Every day of my life, I've wished that things had been different. That even had Anne's diary been lost to the world, Anne and the others might somehow have been saved."

EIGHTEEN

california, 1959–present

Betty saw the movie *The Diary of Anne Frank* when it first came out, and many times afterward. "I thought it was very good," she said. "It showed how tough it was." She couldn't help thinking of Anne in the annex, sitting "quietly" at her "table, before the crack in the window frame," writing: "Let the end come, however cruel."

Betty also went to local productions of the play. She had moved to a little house in Burbank, California. Her sister had divorced and remarried, and lived in Redlands, California. Their mother had passed away in 1967.

Betty held on to the pen-pal letters Anne and Margot had sent to her and Juanita. "I showed them to friends through the years," she recalled, "but nobody got excited until I showed them to Chuck and they rang bells." One night she was having dinner with Chuck (Charles Freedberg), her stockbroker and financial adviser, and her friend Muriel. They were talking about World War II, and Betty mentioned her pen-pal correspondence with the Frank sisters. She pulled out her copy of *The Diary of a Young Girl,* where she now kept the letters, and showed them to Charles. "He couldn't believe what he had in his hands," Betty recalled. "He was the first person I ever showed it to who really got excited." Charles, a Jew active in efforts to remember the victims of the Holocaust, "was awestruck to realize he was holding a letter from Anne Frank," she recalled. His hands started shaking. "You don't know what you have here," he said.

"Charles was very moved," Betty said. "He felt people ought to know about it."

Charles called the Swann Galleries in New York City, known for its specialty in rare books and artifacts, and told a senior cataloger about the pen-pal correspondence. "Too good to be true" was the initial response. George Lowry, president of the galleries, agreed. "I thought it was wild," said Lowry. "I immediately thought of the Hitler diaries—it's a fake." But the director of the Anne Frank House in Amsterdam happened to be in New York and looked at the correspondence. He authenticated all the items. "I know the handwriting well," he said, "and this is it."

The letters from Anne and Margot were the only ones in existence written in English, and were far more valuable than Betty and Juanita had imagined. The Swann Galleries put the pen-pal letters, the envelope in which they came, the picture postcard, and the two small photos of Anne and Margot up for auction. Juanita and Betty planned to give most of the proceeds from the sale to Wayfarers Ministries.

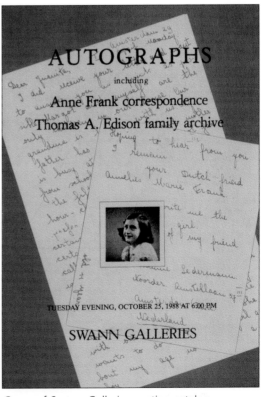

Cover of Swann Galleries auction catalog

On July 23, 1988 the *Redlands Daily Facts* pictured Juanita displaying letters she and Betty received from Anne and Margot.

Although they had had such a hard life themselves, the sisters wanted to help others in need. In 1980 Betty had founded the ministry, a nonprofit organization that shipped books to missionaries all over the world and helped establish libraries in third-world countries.

On July 21, 1988, the Swann Galleries issued a press release announcing the forthcoming sale, and immediately Betty and Juanita were besieged by newspaper reporters and television commentators. The sisters were stunned. "I expected some interest," Betty told a reporter, "but I didn't expect all of this." The phone rang constantly. TV crews showed up on her doorstep. She kept a journal of events that day and the next.

7:00 AM. Ron Bascomb of ABC News called from New York and taped a radio interview.

7:05 AM. Hans Letz of CBS News Los Angeles called to set up an appointment for 10:30 AM to shoot an interview for the Dan Rather evening News.

7:10 AM. Karen Baasignore of Cable News Network (CNN) called and wanted to be here by 9:30 to do a story.

7:25 AM. Willy Rashbaum of United Press International

called to confirm and let me know they wanted to send it to every small town in USA and around the world.

Back in Iowa, everyone was thrilled. "All my friends in Danville buzzed with the news that Betty Ann Wagner had put Danville on the map," Betty wrote.

CBS-TV flew Betty to New York for an appearance on CBS *This Morning*. Juanita could not go with her because she needed to take care of her husband, who had recently suffered a heart attack. She had hoped to visit the Anne Frank House in September but had to cancel that trip as well.

The auction took place on October 25, 1988. A dozen bidders participated, including a Japanese woman, a Los Angeles dentist, and entertainer Whoopi Goldberg. But an anonymous purchaser paid the highest price and bought the correspondence. He then donated the letters, envelope, photos, and postcard to the Simon Wiesenthal Center Library and Archives in Los Angeles.

"We've enjoyed those letters for 48 years," Betty told a reporter, "and now I am happy that they will be enjoyed by others."

An exhibit devoted to the pen-pal correspondence is permanently on view in the Artifacts Room at the Simon Wiesenthal Center—Museum of Tolerance. A message above the entrance to the room reads, *They will always be heard.* For reasons of security and preservation, the originals are stored in a climate-controlled vault. Facsimiles of the

On July 24, 1988, the *Los Angeles Times* pictured Betty holding Anne's letter to Juanita.

From left to right: Anne, Barbara's friend Tineke, Sanne, and Barbara on vacation, Beekbergen, Holland, 1941

Juanita in foreground and Betty on horseback with a neighbor friend, 1941

correspondence appear in a display case along with a first edition of the English-language translation of the diary.

Today Betty hears from new pen pals, especially middle-school students in Iowa. One boy asked, "Did the relationship with Anne and Margot Frank change your life? I would think it did. It certainly would have changed my way of thinking." A girl wrote, "I was surprised to learn that Anne had corresponded with a girl from Iowa before she went into hiding from the war. I just wanted you to know how amazing I think it is that one of the most important figures for World War II had a pen pal from Iowa."

EPILOGUE

Following is a summation of what happened to Anne's pen pals, family, friends, and others involved in her story.

Anne's pen pals:

Juanita Jane Wagner Hiltgen died of a heart attack and diabetes on Christmas Eve 2001, in Redlands, California.

Betty Ann Wagner lives in Burbank, California, where she heads the Wayfarers Ministries, which aids international missionaries and students.

Ann Dunn Wagner passed away in 1967 in California.

Anne's family:

Her sister, Margot Betti Frank, died of typhus in March 1945, at Bergen-Belsen Concentration Camp in Germany.

Her mother, Edith Frank-Holländer, died on January 6, 1945, in Auschwitz Concentration Camp in Poland from weakness and hunger.

Her grandmother Alice Frank-Stern died on March 19, 1953, in Basel, Switzerland.

Her maternal uncles, Walter and Julius Holländer, became United States citizens in 1944, and remained in Leominster, Massachusetts, where they had jobs as factory workers. Neither brother ever married. In 1963 they moved to New York City. On October 4, 1967, Julius died when he fell into an elevator shaft. Walter died less than a year later, on September 19, 1968.

Robert Frank, Otto's older brother, lived in England. Herbert Frank was Otto's younger brother. Anne's aunt Leni (Helene), Otto's sister, married Erich Elias in 1921, and they had two sons, Stephan and Buddy (Bernhard). Buddy Elias is now president of the ANNE FRANK-Fonds in Basel.

Milly Stanfield, Otto's cousin, lived in England and was a cello instructor and music critic. She moved to the United States in 1967.

People in hiding with Anne in the secret annex:

Her roommate, dentist Fritz Pfeffer, was sent from Auschwitz Concentration Camp to the Neuengamme Concentration Camp near

Hamburg, where he died in the sick barracks on December 20, 1944.

Her boyfriend, Peter van Pels, was sent to Auschwitz. Even though Otto wanted Peter to stay with him in the hospital and hide, Peter felt he had a better chance of survival if he left. When the camp was evacuated in mid-January, Peter and the other prisoners were forced to march to Mauthausen Concentration Camp in Austria. He died there on the day of liberation, May 5, 1945, at the age of eighteen.

Peter's mother, Auguste van Pels, was sent from Auschwitz to Bergen-Belsen, where she saw Anne and Margot again. Then she was transferred to Theresienstadt (Terezin) Concentration Camp in Czechoslovakia on April 9,1945, and died sometime between April and May.

Peter's father, Hermann van Pels, was sent to Auschwitz. A month later he injured his thumb while digging a trench and asked to be transferred to indoor work. He was gassed the next day.

The helpers who took care of Anne and the others in hiding:

Miep Gies retired from Opekta and in 1950, at the age of forty-one, gave birth to a son, Paul. She remains in Amsterdam but is too frail to give interviews.

Miep's husband, Jan (Henk) Gies, died in January 1993.

Elisabeth "Bep" Voskuijl left Opekta after the war and married in 1946. She had three sons and a daughter, whom she named Anne, after Anne Frank. In 1959 Bep served as a witness in a legal case in Germany against two neo-Nazis who claimed that the Holocaust never happened and that Anne's diary was a forgery. She stayed in close contact with Otto, who saw to it that she, along with the other "helpers," were honored by *Yad Vashem* memorial in Jerusalem in 1972. Bep died on May 6, 1983, in Amsterdam.

Johannes Kleiman was sent to the Amersfoort Work Camp but was released with the help of the International Red Cross because he suffered from a stomach ailment. In 1944 he went back to work at Opekta and took over the firm when Otto moved to Basel. He died on January 30, 1959.

Victor Gustav Kugler was sent to a number of Holland's work camps but escaped and remained in hiding until the Canadians liber-

ated Holland in May 1945. He emigrated to Toronto, Canada, with
his second wife in 1955 and worked as a bookkeeper. For his partici-
pation in helping the Franks in hiding, he was honored in 1973 by the
Yad Vashem memorial in Jerusalem with the Medal of the Righteous. He
died in Toronto on December 16, 1981.

Anne's friends:

Hannah (Hanneli) Elisabeth Pick-Goslar was sent to Westerbork
Transit Camp in Holland, then to Bergen-Belsen. After the liberation
she and her younger sister, Gabi, the only survivors of their family,
were helped by Otto Frank, and they both emigrated to Palestine (pre-
1948 Israel). Hanneli became a nurse, married a publisher, and had
three children. She still lives in Israel.

Ilse Wagner, a member of Anne's Ping-Pong club, was the first of
the group of Jewish friends to be deported. She was sent to Westerbork
Transit Camp in January 1943, then to the Sobibor Extermination
Camp, and was gassed the day she arrived, April 2, 1943, at the age of
fourteen.

Susanne (Sanne) Ledermann at age fifteen was sent to Westerbork
Transit Camp with her parents. Then they were sent to Auschwitz on
November 19, 1943, and were gassed upon arrival.

Sanne's sister, Barbara Ledermann, joined an underground
Resistance group with her boyfriend when she was seventeen. She
remained in hiding until May 1945, when Canadian troops liberated
Holland. Then she emigrated to the United States in 1947 and later
married Martin Rodbell, a biochemist who shared the 1994 Nobel
Prize for Medicine or Physiology.

Anne's boyfriend Hello Silberberg escaped the Nazi roundups in
Amsterdam, and after the war emigrated to the United States. He now
lives in New Jersey and goes by "Ed," short for Edmond.

Jacqueline van Maarsen was saved by her mother, who secretly took
her daughters to church, had them baptized as Catholics, and talked
the Nazis into changing their status to Aryan. Thus, she also saved
Jacque's father, who, though Jewish, was married to an Aryan. Jacque
later married Ruud Sanders, a Jewish childhood friend who was hid-

den during the war. They live in Amsterdam.

People in Otto's life:

His second wife, Fritzi Geiringer Frank, wrote that her years with Otto were among the happiest of her life. After his death she remained an active member of the Anne Frank Foundation until she became ill in 1993. Her daughter, Eva Geiringer Schloss, took Fritzi to London, where she died in 1998 at the age of ninety-three. Eva still resides in London.

Otto's lifelong friend Nathan Straus, Jr. became an administrator of the United States Housing Authority and a civic leader. He married and had four sons, one of whom, Barnard, vividly remembered Otto's visits to their home in Quarry Lake, New York. Another son, R. Peter Straus, spent a week with Otto and Fritzi in Switzerland in 1974. Nathan Straus, Jr. died in 1961 at the age of seventy-two.

Others:

Karl Josef Silberbauer, the policeman who arrested the Franks, worked for the Vienna police force after the war. He was suspended in 1963 when an investigation began after Simon Wiesenthal tracked him down. Less than a year later the investigation ended for lack of evidence and Silberbauer returned to his post. He died in 1971.

Anne and Margot on the beach. Their father,
Otto, took this picture.

POSTSCRIPT

Anne Frank wrote to Juanita Wagner more than sixty years ago.
When she was cut off from friends and pen pals, she turned to "Kitty,"
her diary, for companionship. To this day the diary of Anne Frank
continues to touch readers everywhere and to stir up debate among
scholars.

Some see the diary as an extraordinary account of a young girl's
understanding of adolescence. Others regard it as a testimony to the
Holocaust. But some critics instead contend that Anne did not write
about the Holocaust; she described the Nazi menace toward Jews that
changed her life and put her in hiding.

Many people learn about Anne through the play or movie based on
the diary. Much controversy still surrounds the original script by
Goodrich and Hackett. Critics claim it overly emphasizes Anne's ide-

alism and glosses over the horror of what really happened to her at the hands of the Nazis. When the play was first produced, only ten years had passed since Anne's death. Many people felt unwilling to face the appalling events that were the background of her writing. But in 2000 playwright Wendy Kesselman wrote a new adaptation of the Goodrich–Hackett play, and both versions remain in print. Although Kesselman retained Anne's concluding remark, "I still believe, in spite of everything, that people are really good at heart," the last scene shows the Nazi officers arresting the Franks and the others in hiding. In a voice-over, Otto tells that they were sent to concentration camps, and he states how the other seven people died. "My daughters' bodies dumped into mass graves, just before the camp is liberated," he says at the end of the play. Then he bends down, picks up Anne's diary, and holding it out to the audience, says, "All that remains."

Anne's life and death have left many unanswered questions. People still wonder about the identity of the betrayer who tipped off the Gestapo. How did Silberbauer know about the secret bookcase? Eyewitnesses testified that he went directly to it and opened the door.

New information has recently surfaced. Author Carol Ann Lee discovered that Anton (Tonny) Ahlers, a Dutch Nazi and violent antisemite, had had business dealings with Otto Frank. Ahlers knew that the Franks and the others were hiding at 263 Prinsengracht, and he made the phone call that prompted the arrest. "He did betray the Frank family," said Ahlers's son, "I am sure of that." Ahlers's brother Casper agreed and said that Tonny seemed "proud of the fact." When the story broke in Holland, it was headline news in the papers and on TV. However, the evidence was circumstantial, so the case is still not closed, and the identity of the betrayer remains uncertain. Ahlers died on August 4, 2000, at the age of eighty-three. That day marked the anniversary of the Franks' arrest.

On the day of the arrest, Silberbauer questioned Miep Gies, but he let her go when he discovered that she was originally from Vienna, just as he was. "She was such a nice girl," he said many years later when cross-examined in a courtroom.

The Dutch regard Miep as a heroine. Queen Beatrix appointed her a knight of the Order of Oranje-Nassau. In 1994 Miep received the Order of Merit of the Federal Republic of Germany, and in Los Angeles, California, was given the Righteous Among the Nations' Laureate award by the Simon Wiesenthal Center and the Museum of Tolerance. The commission for the Righteous of the *Yad Vashem* memorial in Jerusalem bestowed their highest honor on her. However, Miep said, "I am not a hero. I stand at the end of the long, long line of good Dutch people who did what I did or more—much more—during those dark and terrible times years ago. More than twenty thousand Dutch people helped to hide Jews and others in need of hiding during those years. I willingly did what I could to help. My husband did as well. It was not enough."

Over the years, Anne has come to symbolize the 1.5 million Jewish children who were murdered in the Holocaust. Huge numbers of people tour the Anne Frank House. A large proportion of them are American. There have been tributes to Anne from all over the world. Streets have been named for her. But the lessons learned from her diary seem to have had a particularly strong impact on America. In Boise, Idaho, an Anne Frank Human Rights Memorial features a bronze sculpture of Anne holding her diary as she peeps out an imaginary window. Even in Hollywood, the place Anne so much wanted to visit, there is a little garden named for her in the Beth Olam Cemetery.

The Montessori school that she attended in Amsterdam is now called the Anne Frank School. An enlarged replica of her signature is painted on the brick building above the entrance. Inside, a plaque lists the names of all the Jewish children who were sent away from the school in 1941, the names of the concentration camps where they were killed, and the dates of their deaths. Anne Frank is just one of those eighty-one names. But through her diary, stories, and letters, she, her friends, and the other 1.5 million children who perished will always be remembered.

"How wonderful it is that no one has to wait, but can start right now to gradually change the world!"

– Anne Frank, "Give," March 26, 1944

ACKNOWLEDGMENTS

United States

This book started with Juanita and Betty Wagner, and their simple act of friendship when they were young girls. I never had the opportunity to know Juanita, but I did meet and become friends with her sister, Betty. To Betty I owe a huge debt of thanks for sharing family memories, photographs, and an extraordinary archive of material about Anne Frank and the pen- pal correspondence. I also thank Betty for introducing me to Juanita's sons, Robert and Wes Bender, and to her great niece, Christine Bender.

Wes and his wife, Diane, accompanied Betty and me on a memorable research trip to Iowa, where we visited Danville, Burlington, and Iowa City. At the State Historical Society in Iowa City, I particularly thank Kevin Knoot, special collections archivist, for his invaluable assistance throughout this project and Ginalie Swaim, editor, *Iowa Heritage Illustrated*.

My thanks to Betty's relatives Cyrene and Bob Wagner, and to her friends and former classmates Dan and Doris Kelley, Vivian and Don Kellar, and Marjorie Fitzsimmons. At Danville High School I am grateful to Mr. Lynn Jacobson, who gave me his students' project, *Memories of Danville*.

In Los Angeles, California, my research began with my dear partners, Adaire Klein, Director of the Library and Archives at the Simon Wiesenthal Center, and archivist Fama Mor, with whom I worked day and night. I want to express my great appreciation to the following members of their staff: Nancy G. Saul, Margo Gutstein, Susie Mamzhi, and volunteers and translators Jack Voorzanger and Elisabeth Sandler. And my sincere thanks to the Simon Wiesenthal Center and the Museum of Tolerance for their cooperation on this project.

Adaire and Fama introduced me to Leonora Schildkraut, widow of actor Joseph Schildkraut. I thank Leonora for opening her archive to me and spending many hours reviewing carefully preserved audio and visual materials.

In New York I want to acknowledge Joan Adler, Straus family historian, not only for sharing information with me, but for introducing me to Barnard and R. Peter Straus. I thank Peter and Marcia Straus for their hospitality and recollections of the friendship between Nathan Straus, Jr. and Otto Frank.

I am also indebted to Constance Cormier in Leominster, Massachusetts, for providing sources of information concerning Walter and Julius Holländer.

Switzerland

At the ANNE FRANK-Fonds in Basel, I thank Buddy Elias, Anne Frank's cousin, for his cooperation.

The Netherlands

At the Anne Frank House in Amsterdam, I thank Hans Westra, director; Kleis Broekhuizen; Jan van Kooten, head of education; Yt Stoker, collection management; and Teresien da Silva, head of collections, for giving me so much of their time and assistance.

I am grateful to Jacqueline Sanders–van Maarsen and her husband, Ruud, for meeting with me. Talking to Jacqueline deepened my understanding of the true story.

In Amsterdam I am greatly indebted to the following people: Sara van Wassenaer-Matson and her mother-in-law, Louise van Wassenaer-Wiarda; Henny Scheerder and Harry Geelen, and Henny's brother and sister-in-law, Hans and Trix Springer. I also thank author Carol Ann Lee for her help via E-mail. Making new friends like these is one of the great joys of doing research.

This long list would not be complete without an expression of gratitude to my editor, Howard W. Reeves, who instantly understood my vision and made this book a reality. I also want to thank his assistant, Linas Alsenas. And as the cliché goes, last but not least, I give my warmest thanks to George Nicholson, the Center's and my literary agent, for his enthusiasm and tireless devotion to this project. And a big thank-you to *his* assistant, Paul Rodeen.

I close with loving thanks to my close circle of writer friends, who offered their advice and suggestions, and to my son Andy and grandson Marty for their technical assistance, and to my husband, Michael, for his ongoing support.

—Susan Goldman Rubin

In 1988 the Simon Wiesenthal Center Museum of Tolerance Library and Archives became the permanent home of the Anne and Margot Frank pen-pal letters. When the Museum of Tolerance opened in 1993, facsimile copies of the letters were placed on permanent exhibition. My dear colleague Fama Mor took charge of the exhibit as well as the entire archival collection.

For the past ten years, thousands of people have paused to read these poignant letters, wondering about the world and the people, their lives and their hopes.

Our friend, colleague, and partner, Susan Goldman Rubin, provided our first inkling that we could realize our dream. Susan's search for truth, "even unto its innermost parts," combined with the talent of her pen to reach the hearts and souls of readers, has provided us with answers, history, human interest, and photographs. Susan has told the pen-pal story with clarity, honesty, integrity, and, most of all, love. There are no words to adequately express our feelings. May we continue to share dreams and stories for many years to come.

The next step in the realization of our dream was meeting George Nicholson, our literary agent. George came to Los Angeles to visit the Museum of Tolerance and to see the pen-pal exhibition. He immediately became our partner, and we are most appreciative of his commitment and support of our dream. His dedication to the project and to finding the right publisher has been superb, and we are forever grateful.

The final step came with the agreement that Harry N. Abrams, Inc., would publish the book. Howard W. Reeves, director of children's publishing for Abrams, brought his knowledge, experience, support, and commitment to this book. Our heartfelt gratitude to him for his patience and "love" which brings *Searching for Anne Frank: Letters from Amsterdam to Iowa* to the world. And many thanks to Paul Rodeen and Linas Alsenas.

On a personal note, I offer my heartfelt gratitude to the Library and Archives staff—Margo Gutstein, Nancy Saul, Fama Mor, Lisa Engel, and Susie Mamzhi, without whom our dream could not be realized. Together with our loyal cadre of volunteers, they are a very special team. Thank you.

— Adaire Klein
Director of Library and Archival Services
Simon Wiesenthal Center and Museum of Tolerance

The Simon Wiesenthal Center Museum of Tolerance, Los Angeles, California

REFERENCES AND RESOURCES
(*)Denotes materials suitable for younger readers

BOOKS
* Anne Frank House, compilation. *Anne Frank in the World*. New York: Alfred A. Knopf, 2001.

*_____. *The World of Anne Frank*. London: Macmillan, 2001.

*Denenberg, Barry. *The True Story of J. Edgar Hoover and the FBI*. New York: Scholastic, 1993.

Enzer, Hyman A., and Sandra Solotaroff-Enzer, editors. *Anne Frank: Reflections on Her Life and Legacy*. Urbana and Chicago: University of Illinois Press, 2000.

Feingold, Henry L. *Bearing Witness: How America and Its Jews Responded to the Holocaust*. Syracuse, N.Y.: Syracuse University Press, 1995.

*Frank, Anne. *The Diary of a Young Girl: The Definitive Edition*. Edited by Otto H. Frank and Mirjam Pressler. New York: Bantam, Doubleday, Dell, 1991.

*_____. *Anne Frank's Tales from the House Behind*. New York: Bantam Books, 1966.

*_____. *Anne Frank's Tales from the Secret Annex* (previously published in part as *Tales from the House Behind*). New York: Pocket Books, 1982.

_____. *The Diary of Anne Frank: The Critical Edition*. Prepared by the Netherlands State Institute for War Documentation, edited by David Barnouw and Gerrold van der Stroom. Translated by Arnold J. Pomerans and B. M. Mooyaart. New York: Doubleday, 1989. The revised *Critical Edition*. New York: Doubleday, 2003.

Front Page: 100 Years of the Los Angeles Times, *1881–1981*. New York: Harry N. Abrams, 1981.

Garrels, James I., and David R. Gerdes. *The History of the Danville Community*. West Burlington, Iowa: The Des Moines County News, 1966.

*Gies, Miep, with Alison Leslie Gold. *Anne Frank Remembered: The Story of the Woman Who Helped to Hide the Frank Family*. New York: Simon & Schuster, 1987.

* Gilbert, Sir Martin. *The Holocaust: A History of the Jews of Europe During the Second World War*. New York: Henry Holt & Co., 14th printing, 2003.

* Gold, Alison Leslie. *Memories of Anne Frank: Reflections of a Childhood Friend*. New York: Scholastic, 1997.

Hondius, Dienke. *Absent* (Jewish Lyceum Amsterdam, 1941–1943). Amsterdam: Uitgeverij Vassallucci, 2001.

Kopf, Hedda Rosner. *Understanding Anne Frank's* The Diary of a Young Girl. Westport, Conn.: Greenwood Press, 1997.

* Lee, Carol Ann. *The Biography of Anne Frank: Roses from the Earth*. London: Penguin, 1999.

_____. *The Hidden Life of Otto Frank*. London: Viking, 2002.

Lindwer, Willy. *The Last Seven Months of Anne Frank*. New Haven & London: Yale University Press, 1997.

Luick-Thrams, Michael, editor. *Enemies Within: Iowa POWs in Nazi Germany*. Iowa: N.p., 2002.

Melnick, Ralph. *The Stolen Legacy of Anne Frank*. New Haven & London: Yale University Press, 1997.

* Metselaar, Menno, Ruud van der Rol, and Dineke Stam, compilation and editing. *Anne Frank House: A Museum with a Story*. Amsterdam: Anne Frank House, 1999.

Morse, Arthur D. *While Six Million Died*. New York: Random House, 1968.

*Muller, Melissa. *Anne Frank: The Biography*. New York: Henry Holt, 1998.

Ossian, Lisa Lynn. *The Home Fronts of Iowa, 1940–1945*. Ames, Iowa: Iowa State University, 1998.

Page One: Major Events 1920–1988 as Presented in The New York Times. New York: The New York Times Company, 1988.

*Pressler, Mirjam. *Anne Frank: A Hidden Life*. New York: Dutton Children's Books, 1999.

Rosenfeld, Alvin H. "Popularization and Memory: The Case of Anne Frank." *Lessons and Legacies: The Meaning of the Holocaust in a Changing World*, Peter Hayes, editor. Evanston, Ill.: Northwestern University Press, 1991.

*Schloss, Eva, with Evelyn Julia Kent. *Eva's Story: A Survivor's Tale by the Step-sister of Anne Frank*. New York: St. Martin's Press, 1988.

Schnabel, Ernst. *Anne Frank: A Portrait in Courage*. Translated by Richard and Clara Winston. New York: Harcourt, Brace & World, 1958.

*Steenmeijer, Anna G., editor. *A Tribute to Anne Frank*. New York: Doubleday, 1971.

* van der Rol, Ruud, and Rian Verhoeven. *Anne Frank*. Amsterdam: Anne Frank House, 1992.

*van der Rol, Ruud, and Rian Verhoeven for the Anne Frank House. *Anne Frank: Beyond the Diary, a Photographic Remembrance*. New York: Viking, 1993.

*van Maarsen, Jacqueline [Jopie]. *My Friend Anne Frank*. New York: Vantage Press, 1996.

Wagner, Betty Ann, with Dick Ross. *Wayfarers: Pilgrims and Strangers Seek the City Not Made with Hands*. Toluca Lake: Wayfarers Ministries, 1999.

*Wright, Michael, editor. *The World at Arms:* The Reader's Digest *Illustrated History of World War II*. London and New York: Reader's Digest Association Limited, 1989.

Wyman, David S. *The Abandonment of the Jews*. New York: Pantheon Books, 1984.

SCRIPTS OF STAGE PLAYS
*Goodrich, Frances, and Albert Hackett. *The Diary of Anne Frank*. Dramatists Play Service, 1984.

*Kesselman, Wendy. *The Diary of Anne Frank*. Dramatists Play Service, 2001.

ARTICLES
*Bricker, Suzanne. "Not Your Ordinary Pen Pals." *Redlands Daily Facts* (23 July 1988).

"Construction of Iowa Ordnance Plant Here Real Achievement." *The Daily Hawk-Eye Gazette* (31 July 1941).

*Covington, Richard. "Forever Young." Smithsonian (October 2001).

*da Silva, Teresien. "The Secrets of Anne's Room." *Anne Frank Magazine* (2001): 4.

*Johnson, Marilyn. "The Unknown Anne Frank." *Life* 16, no. 7 (June 1993).

Lobdell, George H. "A Tale of Two Christmases at the Algona Prisoner-of-War Camp." *The Palimpsest* (winter 1992).

*Myers-Verhage, Shelby. "Postmarked from Amsterdam—Anne Frank and Her Iowa Pen Pal." *The Palimpsest* (winter 1995).

_____. "The Diaries of Anne Frank and Birdie Mathews." *The Palimpsest* (winter 1995).

"Nathan Straus, 72, Civic Leader and Chairman of WMCA, Dies." *The New York Times* (14 September 1961).

*O' Shaughnessy, Lynn. "Burbank Pen Pal to Share Legacy of Anne Frank." *Los Angeles Times* (24 July 1988).

_____. "Global Interest Stuns Pen Pals of Anne Frank." *Los Angeles Times* (24 July 1988).

Ozick, Cynthia. "Who Owns Anne Frank?" *The New Yorker* (6 October 1997).

Pessar, Henry. *"Franks laererinne ble en tankevekker"* (article about Mrs. Kuperus).

_____. *"La Maestra di Anna Frank Racconta"* (copied at Anne Frank House and translated at the Simon Wiesenthal Center Library).

"Postmarked from Amsterdam: Anne Frank and Her Iowa Pen Pal." *Goldfinch* (spring 1988).

*Sanders-van Maarsen, Jacqueline. "A Friendship in Difficult Times." *Anne Frank Magazine* (2001): 38.

*Shepard, Richard F. "Anne Frank Letter to Iowa Pen Pal to Be Sold." *The New York Times* (21 July 1988).

*Smetak, Jacqueline. "Women on the Home Front: The Iowa WIPEs." *The Palimpsest* (winter 1995).

UNPUBLISHED MANUSCRIPTS

Angress, Dina. *My Autobiography, Including the Second World War Years in Amsterdam, The Netherlands.*

Mathews, Birdie B., 1880–1974, Papers and Travel Diaries. State Historical Society of Iowa, Iowa City.

"Memories of Danville". Collected from 1997–1999. Published by the Danville High School Mass Media Class.

Schildkraut, Joseph. The Joseph Schildkraut Collection of *The Diary of Anne Frank* Memorabilia: Letters, Notes, etc.

Straus, R. Peter. *Her Message Is His Mission: The Father of Anne Frank's Diary.*

Wagner, Betty. *I Remember.*

VIDEOS AND CD-ROMS

Anne Frank. Buena Vista Home Entertainment; directed by Robert Dornhelm, 2001.

Anne Frank House: A House with a Story. Anne Frank House, Hans Westra, general director, 2000.

Anne Frank Remembered. A Jon Blair Film Company production, Columbia Tristar Home Entertainment, 1995.

Betty Wagner: Anne Frank Clips.

The Diary of Anne Frank, Twentieth Century Fox, directed by George Stevens, 1959.

History Through the Lens. "The Diary of Anne Frank: Echoes from the Past." Prometheus Entertainment/Foxstar Productions/Van Ness Films, 2001.

Remembering Anne Frank, with Miep Gies. Anne Frank House, 1998. CD-ROM

WEB SITES
Anne Frank Center, New York:
http://www.annefrank.com

Anne Frank House:
http://www.annefrankhouse.com

Museum of Tolerance Learning Center, Anne Frank:
http://motlc.wiesenthal.org/pages/t022/t02236.html

Simon Wiesenthal Center–Museum of Tolerance Library and Archives
http://www.wiesenthal.com/library

United States Holocaust Memorial Museum, Anne Frank:
www.ushmm.org/wlc/en/index.php?ModuleId=10005210

INTERVIEWS BY THE AUTHOR
Adler, Joan (Straus family historian). Telephone, December 2002.
Angress, Dina. Telephone, 1 April 2002.
Egyedi-Gottel, Kitty. Amsterdam (telephone), May 2002.
Fitzsimmons, Marjorie. Danville, Iowa, 21 September 2002.
Jacobsen, Mr. Lynn. Danville High School, 20 September 2002.
Kellar, Donald and Vivian Kellar (Miss Birdie Mathew's great-nephew and his wife).
   Telephone, 30 April 2002; Burlington, Iowa, 21 September 2002.
Kelley, Dan and Doris Kelley. Danville, Iowa, 21 September 2002.
Ledermann Rodbell, Barbara, North Carolina (telephone), 20 May 2002; 14 October
   2002; 26 December 2002.
Mathews, Cyrene and Bob Mathews. Danville, Iowa, 21 September 2002.
Pick-Goslar, Hannah (Hanneli) Elisabeth. Israel (telephone), 20 May 2002.
Sanders-van Maarsen, Jacqueline. Amsterdam, 29 May 2002.
Scheerder, Henny. Amsterdam, May 29, 2002; The Hague, 31 May 2002.
Schildkraut, Leonora. 19 March 2002; 5 April 2002; 24 April 2002; and 8 May 2002.
Straus, R. Peter and Joan Adler (Straus family historian). New York, 11 February 2003.

van Kooten, Jan. Anne Frank House, Amsterdam, 28 May 2002.

van Wassenaer-Wiarda, Louise. The Hague, 29 May 2002.

Wagner, Betty. Burbank, Calif., 18 January 2002; 8 February 2002; 21 February 2002; 7 March 2002; trip to Iowa, 18 September 2002 to 22 September 2002.

Wagner, Betty and Juanita Wagner Hiltgen's sons, Wes and Robert, and her granddaughter, Christine Bender. Burbank, Calif., 13 April 2002.

ILLUSTRATION CREDITS

(93.102.40)

Page 59 (top): Courtesy National Archives, photo no. 208-PU-95PA-12

Page 61: Maria Austria Instituut, Amsterdam

Page 70: FOUR MOTHERS copyright 1941 Turner Entertainment Co. A Warner Bros. Entertainment Company. All Rights Reserved.

Page 72: Jan Carel Warffemius

Page 75 (top): Courtesy: National Archives, photo no. 65-H-121-1

Page 75 (bottom): Howard Liberman, Library of Congress

Page 78: Copyright ©1944 The New York Times Company. Reprinted by Permission.

Pages 81, 83, 84, 85 (bottom): Netherlands Institute for War Documentation (NIOD)

Page 85 (top): Martin Gilbert, *Holocaust: Maps and Photographs*, 5th edition, Holocaust Educational Trust, London, 1998.

Page 86: The Auschwitz-Birkenau State Museum and the Simon Wiesenthal Center—Museum of Tolerance Library and Archives, Los Angeles

Page 87: Martin Gilbert, *The Atlas of Jewish History*, 6th edition. London and New York: Routledge, 2003.

Page 89: Hadassah Bimko Rosensaft, Courtesy: United States Holocaust Memorial Museum

Page 93: United States Holocaust Memorial Museum, courtesy of Jack and Iris Mitchell Bolton

Page 97: Photograph courtesy of Buddy Elias, private collection

Page 105: Photo copyright Maria Austria Instituut, Amsterdam

Page 106: Courtesy: The Joseph Schildkraut Archives

Page 107: Maria Austria Instituut, Amsterdam, and The Joseph Schildkraut Archives

Page 108: Harry Ransom Humanities Research Center, The University of Texas at Austin

Page 111 (bottom), 119: Courtesy: Simon Wiesenthal Center—Museum of Tolerance Library and Archives, Los Angeles, and from the Collection of Betty Wagner

Page 113: Twentieth Century Fox and The Joseph Schildkraut Archives

Page 115: Simon Wiesenthal Center—Museum of Tolerance Library and Archives, Los Angeles, and *Anne Frank Remembered*, by Miep Gies and Alison Leslie Gold. New York: Simon & Schuster, 1987.

Page 120: Rick Sforza/*Redlands Daily Facts*

Page 121: George Wilhelm, Copyright 2003, *Los Angeles Times*. Reprinted with permission.

INDEX